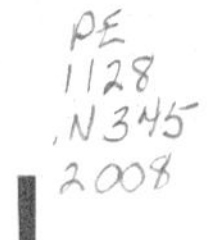

Ramona's Adventure

Elizabeth Neblett

Modern Dramas 4: Ramona's Adventure
First Edition

Pearson Education, Inc.
10 Bank Street, White Plains, NY 10606

Staff credits: The people who made up the ***Modern Dramas 4: Ramona's Adventure*** team, representing editorial, production, design, and manufacturing, include Pietro Alongi, Andrea Bryant, Dave Dickey, Ann France, Laura Le Dréan, Martha McGaughey, Jaime Lieber, Michael Mone, Edie Pullman, and Mary Rich.

Cover illustration: Chris Pavely
Text design: Jimmie Young, Tolman Creek Design
Text composition: S4 Carlisle Publishing Services
Text font: 12.5/13 Minion
Illustrations: Chris Pavely

ISBN-13: 978-0-13-513180-0
ISBN-10: 0-13-513180-4

Printed in the United States of America
6 7 8 9 10 V056 16 15

Contents

To the Teacher

Ramona's Adventure is the fourth and last book in the series of four Longman *Modern Dramas*. These dramas provide authentic, level-appropriate, engaging literature for adult English language learners. The individual episodes of the books can either stand alone or be taught in sequence as part of an ongoing course. *Modern Dramas* fill the need in the beginning to low-intermediate classroom for controlled reading material of more than a few paragraphs. *Modern Dramas* also keep the students interested in what they are reading: They will want to keep turning the pages to find out what happens next.

You will be amazed at how engaged your students will be with these stories. The involving story lines will draw students in, and motivate them to keep on reading. The language is not completely grammatically controlled; *Modern Dramas* aim above all to be interesting and natural, and have been written with an eye to research that shows that most students' reading ability is at a higher level than their speaking, listening, or writing skills. By the last Episode, your students will be able to follow the plot and to answer the reading comprehension questions without using their dictionaries.

In this last book of the series, eleven episodes follow the story of Ramona as she copes with the challenges of balancing her business, her family, and her personal life. Students learn vocabulary related to traveling, health issues, and relationships.

Each of the eleven Episodes consists of:

- **The opening page**
  A picture sparks student interest in the Episode to come, and provides a springboard for lively student discussion.
- **Get Ready to Read**
  The three questions about the opening art can be discussed in pairs, small groups, or with the whole class. These questions focus students' attention on the theme of the episode. An exercise after these questions introduces new vocabulary.
- **In the last episode**
  Each episode starts with a brief summary of the previous episode, so that students who were absent will be able to follow the story, and students who have been in class will be reminded of what has already happened.

- **The reading**
  Each reading is between 600 and 1,000 words. You can assign the episode and the exercises following it for homework, but it is also useful to read it aloud to the class, or to have the students listen to the recording of the episode before they read it on their own. New vocabulary not targeted on the opening page is defined with a gloss on the relevant page.
- **Reading Comprehension**
  These true/false, fill-in, short answer, and multiple-choice questions check students' understanding of what they have just read. The exercises can be used for class discussion. You can encourage students to explain their answers or tell the class where in the episode they found the information to answer the questions.
- **Work with the Words**
  These exercises review and solidify students' knowledge of new vocabulary, both the words targeted on the opening page and other vocabulary words which have come up in the reading. The exercises are multiple choice, fill in the blank, and select the opposite word, among others.
- **Lifeskill Practice**
  These exercises focus on a particular theme or competency featured in the episode. The exercises reinforce standard life skills and competencies.
- **Dialogue Practice**
  Selected portions of the episode are reproduced at the end of each of the nine segments so that students can practice the language in a focused way. These can be used for pronunciation practice or role play.

After your students finish *Ramona's Adventure*, they will be eager to read the other books in the *Modern Dramas* series: *Solomon the Superintendent*, *Lucy and the Piano Player*, and *Victor's Secret.*

The Phone Call

Get Ready to Read

A **Discuss with a partner.**

1. Do you buy flowers?
2. Is there a florist shop in your neighborhood? What does it look like?
3. What does the store sell in addition to flowers?

B **Match the words and expressions with the definitions.**

d	1. grown	a. have a new opinion
____	2. widow	b. not tell the truth
____	3. change her mind	c. have a good relationship with
____	4. run (a business)	d. adult; not a child or teenager
____	5. lie	e. not big; fit close to the body
____	6. tight (clothes)	f. manage
____	7. get along with	g. a woman whose husband died

About Ramona

Ramona Rivera is a **widow**. She has a business, a florist shop called Family Flowers in Elizabeth, New Jersey. Ramona started the business with her husband. After he died five years ago, Ramona thought, "Maybe I should sell the shop. I can't **run** the business alone," but she **changed her mind**. She has many regular customers and four **employees**.* They all work hard, but Ramona likes to go to work every day. The business is doing very well now.

Ramona is originally from Mexico, but when she was four years old her family immigrated to San Antonio, Texas. When she was 20 years old, she got married and moved with her husband, Fernando, to New Jersey. Ramona's mother, Lourdes, and her sister, Isabel, moved from Texas back to Mexico three years ago. Ramona is close to her mother and sister and visits them often, but her life is in New Jersey. She doesn't want to move back to Mexico. Ramona has three beautiful **grown** children, and two of them live close to her. Her oldest son, Fernando, or "Nando," is 34 and lives in Elizabeth with his wife and children. Ramona's middle child, Ernesto, is 33. He's single and lives in Los Angeles, California. Margarita is the youngest in the family. She's 29, and she's engaged. Margarita lives with Ramona and their small dog, Mambo, in the two-family house that Ramona and her husband bought many years ago. Ramona rents out the apartment on the second floor.

Ramona is 55 years old, but she looks younger. She's an attractive woman. When people meet her, they are surprised to hear that Ramona has grown children because she looks very young.

*__employee__ = someone who works for someone else (**employer** = the boss)

It's two o'clock in the afternoon, and Ramona is at her florist shop. She's talking to Nelly, an employee who also is her best friend.

"So, Ramona, are you busy on Saturday night?" asks Nelly.

"Not really, Nelly. Why?" asks Ramona.

"Well, I'm going to have a small party. It's my husband's birthday. Would you like to come?"

"Sure. Can I bring something to eat?"

"No, don't bring anything. But wear your blue dress," says Nelly.

Ramona looks confused. "Why? That dress is too **tight**."

Nelly laughs. "No, it's not. It's perfect. You look great in that dress. I want you to meet a friend."

Now Ramona looks angry. "Not again, Nelly! Do you remember the last time you did this? That man wasn't looking for a relationship—he was looking for a nurse! And he was 80 years old!"

Nelly says, "I'm sorry about that. He **lied** about his age. I thought he was 70. Relax, Ramona. This man is very nice. He's tall, has dark hair, and he's very attractive. He's a dentist. You'll **get along with** him very well."

Ramona says, "No, thanks. I think I'll stay home and watch TV. I'm not interested in meeting anyone right now. Now, let's talk about the flowers for the Carter wedding."

"Come on, Ramona. That wedding is four months away. Listen, Fernando has been dead for five years. It's time for you to meet someone new. You're still young and attractive, and . . ." The phone on the counter rings.

"Excuse me, Nelly. We can talk about this later. Hello, Family Flowers."

It's Ramona's sister, calling from Mexico.

"Hi, Isabel. What's new?"

Suddenly, Ramona looks upset. "What? When? OK, OK. Relax. I'll be there as soon as I can. I'll call the airline right now."

Nelly looks worried. "What happened, Ramona? Is everything OK?"

Ramona says, "That was my sister, Isabel. My mother just had a **stroke.*** She's in intensive care at the hospital in Manzanillo. I have to go to Mexico right away. Can you run the shop for me for a few weeks?"

Nelly nodded. "Of course. Go home and **pack.**** Call me when you get there. I hope your mother's OK."

Ramona needs to go home to pack for her trip, but first she calls her friend, Selima. Selima is a travel agent.

"Leisure Travel. Selima speaking. May I help you?"

"Selima, this is Ramona."

"Hi, Ramona, how are you?"

"Not so good. My mother's sick and I need to go to Mexico today."

"Of course, Ramona," says Selima. "I'll do it for you. Where do you need to go? I'll book your flight. We have your credit card information on file."

"I'm going to Manzanillo. There isn't a direct flight from Newark, but I can get a nonstop to Houston and then change planes there."

"I'll do my best. Are you at home?"

Ramona answers, "No, I'm at the shop, but I'm leaving right now. I have to pack and make a few phone calls."

"OK. I'll call you at home when I have the reservation."

"Thanks, Selima. Talk to you later."

Ramona hangs up the phone. Then she gets her purse and says good-bye to Nelly. Nelly gives Ramona a big hug.

*stroke = a sudden serious illness in the brain

**pack = put clothes and other things into a suitcase before a trip. (unpack = take things out of the suitcase after arrival.)

Reading Comprehension

A Circle *True* or *False*.

1. Ramona is divorced.	**True**	**False**
2. Ramona lives with her daughter, Mambo.	**True**	**False**
3. Ramona lives in New Jersey.	**True**	**False**
4. Some of Ramona's family lives in Mexico.	**True**	**False**
5. Ramona never visits her mother and sister.	**True**	**False**
6. Ramona started the business by herself.	**True**	**False**
7. Nelly thinks Ramona needs to start dating again.	**True**	**False**
8. Ramona is interested in meeting Nelly's friend.	**True**	**False**

B Circle the correct answer.

1. How does Ramona feel after the phone call?

a. She's happy.
b. She's upset.
c. She feels good.
d. She feels tired.

2. Who's going to run the shop for Ramona?

a. Mambo
b. her daughter, Margarita
c. her husband
d. Nelly

3. Who does Ramona call after she talks to her sister?

a. a travel agent
b. her children
c. her mother
d. her neighbor

4. Which flights does Ramona want?

a. Newark to Mexico City
b. Newark to Mexico City; Mexico City to Manzanillo
c. Newark to Houston, Texas; Houston to Manzanillo
d. Newark to Manzanillo nonstop

C **Complete the information about Ramona and her family.**

Ramona is 55 years old. Her ______________ died five years ago. She owns a ______________ shop.

Ramona has three ______________. She has two ______________ and one ______________. One son's name is ______________. He lives with his wife and ______________. Her middle son's name is ______________. Her ______________'s name is ______________. She lives with Ramona.

Work with the Words

A **Circle the correct answer.**

1. I thought I wanted chocolate ice cream, but then I ________ and got vanilla.
   - **a.** changed my mind
   - **b.** got along
   - **c.** did well
   - **d.** ran the ice cream shop
2. Ramona and Nelly **get along with** each other well. They are ________.
   - **a.** friends
   - **b.** neighbors
   - **c.** family
   - **d.** not friendly
3. Mrs. Lee is a **widow**. Her ________ died last year.
   - **a.** mother
   - **b.** grandfather
   - **c.** husband
   - **d.** sister
4. Mrs. Lee's children are **grown**. They are ________.
   - **a.** adults
   - **b.** in elementary school
   - **c.** not working
   - **d.** tall
5. I am an **employee** at National Foods Supermarket. I ________ there.
   - **a.** live
   - **b.** shop
   - **c.** have an account
   - **d.** work

6. He said he was a doctor, but he wasn't. He ________.
   a. changed his mind
   b. got along
   c. ran the business
   d. lied

B Complete the sentences with the correct words and phrases.

employee	get along with	lies	tight
employer	grown	stroke	widow

1. I ______________ all of my neighbors. We have parties together.
2. Only one ______________ is working at the florist today.
3. Ramona's mother is in the hospital because she had a ______________.
4. Mrs. Lee is a ______________. Now she lives alone.
5. Her children are ______________, so now she can travel.
6. I didn't want to wear the jeans because they were very ______________.
7. James is not honest. He ______________ a lot.
8. I have a great ______________. I get five weeks of vacation every year.

C Complete the sentences with the correct words.

her **his** **my** **our** **their** **your**

1. Ramona changed ______________ mind.
2. I changed ______________ mind.
3. Ernesto changed ______________ mind.
4. My wife and I changed ______________ minds.
5. My children changed ______________ minds.
6. You changed ______________ mind.

Lifeskill Practice

■ Make a plane reservation

Complete the conversation with the correct words and phrases. Then practice the conversation with a classmate.

come back	**expiration date**	**nonstop**	**reservation**
credit card	**leave**	**planes**	

A: May I help you?

B: Hi, I'd like to make a plane ______________. I need to go from San Francisco to Lubbock, Texas.

A: When would you like to travel?

B: I want to ______________ tomorrow and ______________ on Sunday. Are there any ______________ flights to Lubbock?

A: No, but I can get you a ______________ flight from San Francisco to Los Angeles. Then you have to change ______________ for Lubbock.

B: That sounds OK.

A: May I have your ______________ number with the ______________, please?

Dialogue Practice

Practice the conversation with a classmate.

Nelly: So, Ramona, are you busy on Saturday night?

Ramona: Not really, Nelly. Why?

Nelly: Well, I'm going to have a small party. It's my husband's birthday. Would you like to come?

Ramona: Sure. Can I bring something to eat?

Nelly: No, don't bring anything. But wear your blue dress.

Ramona: Why? That dress is too tight.

Nelly: (*laughing*) No, it's not. It's perfect. You look great in that dress. I want you to meet a friend.

Ramona: (*angrily*) Not again, Nelly! Do you remember the last time you did this? That man wasn't looking for a relationship—he was looking for a nurse! And he was 80 years old!

Nelly: I'm sorry about that. He lied about his age. I thought he was 70. Relax, Ramona. This man is very nice. He's tall, has dark hair, and he's very attractive. He's a dentist. You will get along with him very well.

Ramona: No, thanks. I think I'll stay home and watch TV. I'm not interested in meeting anyone right now. Now, let's talk about the flowers for the Carter wedding.

Nelly: Come on, Ramona. That wedding is four months away. Listen, Fernando has been dead for five years. It's time for you to meet someone new.

Getting Ready to Go Home

Get Ready to Read

A **Discuss with a partner.**

1. Why is Ramona packing?
2. How does she feel right now?
3. When is she going to leave?

B **Match the words and expressions with the definitions.**

f	1. give someone a ride	a. a plan of a trip
____	2. check in	b. busy traffic time, when people are going to work or going home
____	3. take care of	c. watch; supervise
____	4. landlord	d. excited; nervous
____	5. itinerary	e. register for an airplane flight
____	6. rush hour	f. take someone in your car
____	7. anxious	g. person who owns a building or house and rents space to other people

In the last episode...

Ramona is a florist in New Jersey. She is a widow and has three grown children. She has a good life, but right now she is very upset because her sister, Isabel, just called her from Mexico. Her sister told her that their mother was in the hospital, so Ramona is preparing for a trip to Mexico. Ramona's family is originally from Mexico, and her mother and sister moved back there about three years ago.

Ramona is worried about her mother. Thirty minutes ago, her sister, Isabel, telephoned. She told Ramona that their mother had a stroke, and now their mother is in the hospital. Ramona is very **anxious**. She's packing a small suitcase. She also needs to make some telephone calls. First, she calls her daughter, Margarita, on her cell phone. Margarita is a physician's assistant at the local hospital. She didn't answer her cell phone, so Ramona is waiting for Margarita to call back. Ramona's phone rings. She answers it right away.

"Hello?"

"Ramona, this is Selima. I made a reservation for you. You forgot to tell me when you're coming back."

"Can I leave it open? I don't know how long I'm going to be there."

"Sure, Ramona, but it will be more expensive."

"That's OK. This is important. Can I pick up the tickets now?"

"Do you have a computer at home, Ramona?"

"Yes, I do. Why?"

"I'll e-mail you an e-ticket and your **itinerary**. You can print your ticket and boarding pass at home."

"Great. Thanks so much. What time does the flight leave?"

"Your flight leaves at six o'clock. Try to be at the airport at four o'clock, and don't forget your passport."

"I won't. Thanks, Selima. I'll talk to you when I get back."

"Take care, Ramona. I hope your mother's OK."

"Thanks. See you in a few weeks." Ramona hangs up and continues to pack.

Ramona's phone rings again. This time it's her daughter, Margarita, calling her back. She's worried, because Ramona never calls her at work.

"Mommy, what happened?" asks Margarita. "You never call me at work. What's wrong?"

"Margarita, I have some bad news. Grandma Lourdes is in the hospital. Aunt Isabel called me a couple of hours ago, so I'm packing now, and I have a flight at six o'clock this evening. Can you **give me a ride** to the airport? I have to be there at four o'clock."

"Slow down. You're talking too fast, Mommy. Why is Grandma in the hospital?"

"She had a stroke. She's in intensive care. I have to get there right away."

"Oh, no! I can't believe it. Grandma Lourdes was always so strong. But, Mommy, I can't come home. There was a school bus accident a few minutes ago, and the emergency room is **crazy**.* I have to stay. Maybe Mr. Martinez can drive you to the airport."

"That's a good idea, Margarita. I'll ask him right now. I think he's at home. If not, I'll call a taxi."

"I'm sorry, Mommy."

"That's all right. Just make sure you **take care of** everything while I'm in Mexico. Nelly's going to take care of the store. You'll have to watch Mambo. I'll feed her and walk her before I leave. She'll be OK tonight, but don't forget about her."

"Don't worry, Mommy," promises Margarita.

"Good. I have to go, Margarita. I'll call you when I get to Manzanillo. Oh, and call your brothers, Margarita. I don't have time to call them."

"I'll call Nando and Ernesto. Don't worry. Bye, Mommy. Give a kiss to Grandma and Aunt Isabel for me."

"Bye, sweetie. I'll talk to you soon." Ramona hangs up the phone. She feels a little better, but she's still worried.

It's 3:30 in the afternoon. Upstairs, Ramona's tenant, Mr. Martinez, is checking his students' homework. Mr. Martinez teaches chemistry at a high school in Newark. Every night before dinner, he checks his students' homework assignments and prepares for the next day. He has lived in Ramona's house for five years. He is a good tenant, and he thinks that Ramona is a good **landlord**. She and her daughter are friendly and everyone gets along well together. Mr.

*__crazy__ = very busy

Martinez helps Ramona take care of the garden, and sometimes he watches Mambo when Ramona and her daughter are away. He is divorced and has a 20-year-old son named Miguel, but Miguel doesn't live at home. He's away at college in Massachusetts.

Mr. Martinez hears a knock at the door.

"Who is it?" he asks.

"It's Ramona Rivera, Mr. Martinez."

He opens the door. "Hello, Mrs. Rivera. How are you today?"

"I'm sorry to bother you, Mr. Martinez, but I have a family emergency. My mother had a stroke, and I have to go to Mexico right away. If it's not too much trouble, could you give me a ride to the airport?"

"Of course I can. Are you ready to go now? Let me get my keys. I'm so sorry to hear about your mother."

Mr. Martinez and Ramona arrive at the airport at 3:50. There was heavy traffic on the way to the terminal because it's **rush hour**, but Ramona is glad that she lives close to the airport. It **took*** only 20 minutes to get to the airport. Mr. Martinez is taking Ramona's suitcase out of the **trunk**.**

"Here you are, Mrs. Rivera. Is there anything I can do for you?" he asked.

"Oh, yes, Mr. Martinez. My daughter will be at home later, but could you check on Mambo? Here is an extra set of keys. Sometimes Margarita has to work

***took (20 minutes)** = The trip started at 3:30 and ended at 3:50.

****trunk** = storage area in the back part of a car

long hours. Here's her cell phone number. Also, Mambo needs some **company**,* and she needs to go for a walk a couple of times a day."

"I know, Mrs. Rivera. Don't you worry. I'll take care of everything. Have a safe trip. I hope everything's OK with your family."

"Thanks so much, Mr. Martinez." Ramona takes her suitcase and gets in line to **check in**. A police officer beeps his horn at Mr. Martinez to tell him to move his car.

"OK, OK. I'm moving. I'm moving." Mr. Martinez pulls away from the curb and drives home.

Reading Comprehension

A Circle *True* or *False.*

1. Ramona is packing a suitcase.	True	False
2. Mambo is going to Mexico with Ramona.	True	False
3. Selima is going to e-mail Ramona's ticket.	True	False
4. Ramona called Margarita at work.	True	False
5. Margarita is a nurse.	True	False
6. Ramona calls Margarita at work every day.	True	False
7. Margarita is going to Mexico with her mother.	True	False
8. Margarita is going to call her brothers.	True	False

B Circle the correct answer.

1. Who's going to feed Ramona's dog?
   - **a.** Nelly
   - **b.** Margarita
   - **c.** Mr. Martinez
   - **d.** both b and c

2. Margarita can't drive Ramona to the airport because ________.
   - **a.** she doesn't have a car
   - **b.** she has an appointment
   - **c.** she's at work and can't leave
   - **d.** her car is not working

*__company__ = a friend who visits and spends time with someone

3. It takes ________ for Ramona to get to the airport.
   a. about 20 minutes
   b. 30 minutes
   c. one hour
   d. more than an hour
4. Why did Ramona give Mr. Martinez a set of keys before she left?
   a. He's going to walk the dog.
   b. He lost his keys.
   c. She doesn't want to take the keys to Mexico.
   d. She wants him to give the keys to her daughter.

C Complete the information about Mr. Martinez.

alone	**dog**	**high**	**Miguel**	**teacher**
divorced	**garden**	**is**	**son**	**tenant**

Mr. Martinez is Ramona's ______________. He lives ______________ on the second floor of the house. He's ______________, and he is a chemistry ______________ at a ______________ school in Newark. Sometimes, Mr. Martinez takes care of Ramona's ______________. He also sometimes feeds her ______________. He has one ______________. His name is ______________. He ______________ 20 years old.

Work with the Words

A Circle the correct answer.

1. When I **check in** at the airport, I need ________.
   a. some water
   b. a boarding pass
   c. a ticket
   d. both b and c
2. A ________ rents apartments to other people.
   a. landlord
   b. tenant
   c. neighbor
   d. travel agent

3. I feel **anxious** when ________.
   a. I watch TV
   b. I take an exam
   c. I have a day off from work
   d. I get up in the morning

4. A friend is going to **give me a ride** because ________.
   a. my car is not working
   b. I have a new car
   c. she doesn't have a car
   d. she was in an accident

5. A **physician's assistant** works in a ________.
   a. hospital
   b. school
   c. travel agency
   d. both a and b

6. My mother lives alone, so she likes to have a dog for ________.
   a. company
   b. conversation
   c. work
   d. help

7. My friend sent me an **e-mail** ________.
   a. for my birthday present
   b. to say hello
   c. for $25
   d. package

8. Ramona **takes care of** ________.
   a. her plants
   b. her grandmother
   c. her children
   d. a, b, and c

9. I don't like to travel at **rush hour** because ________.
   a. there is too much traffic
   b. I feel lonely
   c. there are no buses
   d. the weather is bad

10. My father knows where I am every day of my trip because I gave him my ________.
    a. e-mail address
    b. cell phone number
    c. ticket
    d. itinerary

11. His office was **crazy** yesterday. He ________.
    a. didn't have time to eat lunch
    b. went to sleep
    c. answered the phone
    d. went to the hospital

B Complete the sentences with the correct words. You do not need all the words.

anxious	**company**	**e-mail**	**landlord**	**take care of**
check in	**crazy**	**give me a ride**	**rush hour**	

1. A classmate is going to ______________ because it's raining very hard tonight.
2. My window is broken. I need to call my ______________.
3. I'm going to ______________ at the airline counter and give the agent my suitcase.
4. I am always ______________ when I go to the doctor's office.
5. He always tries to leave the office early. He doesn't like to drive during ______________.
6. If you don't have time to call, ______________ me the information.
7. During my vacation, my neighbor will ______________ my plants. She will water them a few times a week.
8. Dogs are lonely when their owners leave. They really need to have ______________.

C Read the answers. Write the questions.

1. **Q:** *How long does it take* to get to the airport?
   A: It takes 20 minutes.
2. **Q:** ______________ to have dinner?
   A: It takes 30 minutes.
3. **Q:** ______________ to drive to your office?
   A: It takes 45 minutes.

Lifeskill Practice

Ask for a favor politely

Ramona asks Mr. Martinez: "If it's not too much trouble, could you give me a ride to the airport?" He answers, "Of course I can." To refuse, we say, "I'm sorry, I can't right now."

A: If it's not too much trouble, could you help me with my homework?

B: Of course, I can. OR I'm sorry, but I can't right now.

A: If it's not too much trouble, could you paint the garage?

B: Of course, I can. OR I'm sorry, but I can't right now.

Write your own conversation. Ask a favor. Then practice with a classmate.

A: If it's not too much trouble, could you ________________?

B: Of course, I can. OR I'm sorry, but I can't right now.

Dialogue Practice

Practice the conversation with a classmate.

Margarita: Mommy, what happened? You never call me at work. What's wrong?

Ramona: Margarita, I have some bad news. Grandma Lourdes is in the hospital. Aunt Isabel called me a couple of hours ago, so I'm packing now, and I have a flight at six o'clock this evening. Can you give me a ride to the airport? I have to be there at four o'clock.

Margarita: Slow down. You're talking too fast, Mommy. Why is Grandma in the hospital?

Ramona: She had a stroke. She's in intensive care. I have to get there right away.

Margarita: Oh, no! I can't believe it. Grandma Lourdes was always so strong. But, Mommy, I can't come home. There was a school bus accident a few minutes ago, and the emergency room is crazy. I have to stay. Maybe Mr. Martinez can drive you to the airport.

Ramona: That's a good idea, Margarita. I'll ask him right now. I think he's at home. If not, I'll call a taxi.

Margarita: I'm sorry, Mommy.

Ramona: That's all right.

At the Hospital

Get Ready to Read

A **Discuss with a partner.**

1. Who is Ramona hugging?
2. Where are they going to go now?
3. How are they feeling?

B **Match the words with the definitions.**

_b_ **1.** afraid		**a.** go fast; hurry
____ **2.** recover		**b.** frightened
____ **3.** look like		**c.** right now
____ **4.** miss		**d.** good at a job or other things; helpful
____ **5.** immediately		**e.** get better
____ **6.** responsible		**f.** feel sad about something or someone that is not there
____ **7.** rush		**g.** have a similar face

In the last episode...

Ramona is traveling to Mexico to see her mother, Lourdes. Lourdes is in intensive care at a hospital in Manzanillo because she had a stroke. Ramona took a flight from Newark at six o'clock. Her neighbor and tenant, Mr. Martinez, took her to the airport. Her friends and family are going to take care of everything while she's away.

It's eleven o'clock, and Ramona is waiting at the baggage claim area for her sister to **pick her up**.* The airport is quiet because it's late. The flight was on time, but Ramona is tired, and she's worried about her mother, too. Suddenly, she hears her name.

"Ramona, Ramona!" It's Isabel, Ramona's older sister.

"Isabel!" Ramona and Isabel hug and kiss. They both begin to cry.

"I **missed** you, Ramona," says Isabel. Isabel feels better with Ramona there. Ramona is two years younger, but she's very **responsible**, and she always knows what to do. Ramona **looks like** Isabel. Everyone always knows that they are sisters.

"I missed you, too," Ramona says. "How's Mami?"

"She's in serious condition, but she is talking a little. She's very lucky. We were at the market when it happened. An ambulance came very quickly and took her to my hospital **immediately**," says Isabel. Isabel is a nurse at a local hospital.

"That's good. We are lucky that you are a nurse. I want to see her," says Ramona. "Can we go to the hospital now?"

"It's late. Visiting hours are over, but I know the head nurse. Let's go," says Isabel.

Thirty minutes later, Ramona and Isabel are at the hospital. It's a small hospital, but it's good. There is a medical school across from the main building. Ramona and Isabel **rush** to the intensive care unit. Ramona is nervous because she's **afraid** of hospitals. When they arrive at the reception desk, a nurse stops them. She knows Isabel. "I'm sorry, Isabel. Visiting hours are over."

***pick her up** = meet someone (at the airport, or anywhere), usually with a car

Ramona cries, "But I came all the way from New Jersey. I need to see my mother tonight!"

"Come on, Nina," says Isabel. "You know me. This is my sister, Ramona. Can we visit for a few minutes? Ramona wants to see her."

"OK. You can stay for five minutes," says Nina.

They go into the intensive care unit. Ramona's mother is sleeping.

Ramona is more upset when she sees her mother, Lourdes, in her hospital room. There are many machines and tubes around the bed. An **IV**[*] is in her right arm.

"Isabel," Ramona takes her sister's hand and **whispers**,[**] "Tell me the truth. You're a nurse. How is she?"

"Ramona, I'm a **surgical nurse.**[†] I don't know very much about strokes, but I do know that we are lucky. Time is very important in cases like this. Mami was at the hospital only 30 minutes after it happened. The doctor says that she's going to recover, but it might take a little time."

"Can she speak? Remember Grandma Ana? She had a stoke, and she couldn't speak after that."

"That was different, Ramona. Mami is younger than Grandma Ana was."

Suddenly, their mother moves in her bed and opens her eyes.

"Mami?" says Ramona. "Are you **awake**?"[††]

Slowly, Lourdes opens her eyes. "I was trying to sleep, but you girls are talking too much. Ramona? Is that you? What are you doing here?"

"Isabel called me, and I arrived 30 minutes ago. How do you feel?"

"A little better, but tired. Ramona, what about the flower shop? Who's taking care of the business?"

"Don't worry, Mami. Nelly's taking care of everything. I'm going to stay here for a while. I want to talk to the doctor. What's his name?"

Isabel says, "Ramona, relax. Everything is fine. We have a good doctor. Doctor Valenzuela is a friend of the family. We have an appointment with him tomorrow morning at 8:30. He'll meet us here."

[*]**IV** = medical equipment (a needle) that puts liquid directly into the body through a vein (intravenous)

[**]**whisper** = speak in a soft voice

[†]**surgical nurse** = nurse who works in the operating room

[††]**awake** = not sleeping

Nina the nurse walks in. "I'm sorry, but your mother needs rest. We'll take good care of her."

"All right," Ramona says. "I'll see you tomorrow, Mami." She kisses her mother on the cheek.

"See you tomorrow, Ramona. You, too, Isabel."

"Good night, Mami," says Isabel. As they leave, Isabel speaks to Nina, "Thanks, Nina. My sister feels much better now."

"You're welcome," says Nina.

The next morning at 8:15, Ramona and Isabel are sitting in their mother's hospital room. They didn't get much sleep because they were thinking about their mother, and they spent most of the night talking. When they arrive at the hospital, they speak to the nurse at the desk. It's a different nurse, and she says that their mother had a good night. She slept well. They hear the doctor coming.

"Good morning, Doctor," says the nurse.

"Good morning, Linda," says the doctor, "May I see Mrs. Cruz's chart, please?"

The doctor walks into the room. "Good morning, Isabel." Then he looks at Ramona and shakes her hand, "I'm Dr. Valenzuela. How do you do?"

"How do you do? I'm Ramona Rivera, her other daughter."

Ramona is surprised. The doctor is young. He looks about 35. He's about the same age as her son, Fernando. He's very handsome.

"How is she, Doctor?" asks Ramona.

"I checked her chart. She had a good night. Your mother is **recovering** well. She is receiving excellent care. We're going to do some tests this morning."

"What kind of tests?" asks Lourdes. She's awake.

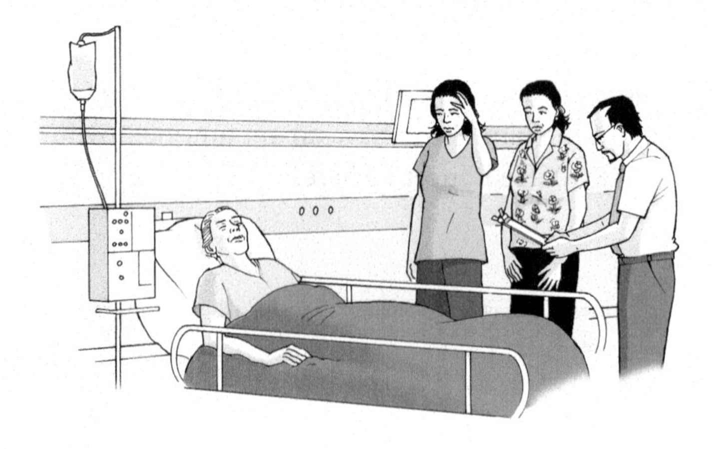

"Good morning, Mrs. Cruz," says the doctor. "How are you feeling?"

"Well, I'm feeling . . . " answers Lourdes. Then she stops talking. A machine begins to beep.

"Mami! Mami! Doctor, what's happening?" asks Isabel.

Dr. Valenzuela goes to the other side of the bed. He's looking at the machines. "Get the nurse!" he shouts to Isabel.

Reading Comprehension

A Circle *True* or *False.*

1. Ramona's flight is late.	**True**	**False**
2. Ramona can't see her mother until the next morning.	**True**	**False**
3. The nurse gives Ramona a little time to visit.	**True**	**False**
4. Isabel is a nurse in the intensive care unit.	**True**	**False**
5. Ramona's mother is surprised to see her.	**True**	**False**
6. At first, Ramona's mother is feeling better.	**True**	**False**
7. The doctor is a member of their family.	**True**	**False**
8. The night nurse says the sisters can stay longer.	**True**	**False**

B Circle the correct answer.

1. Who didn't sleep well last night?

a. Lourdes
b. Ramona
c. Isabel
d. both b and c

2. Why didn't Ramona sleep well?

a. She was tired.
b. She didn't feel well.
c. She had a headache.
d. She talked most of the night with her sister.

3. Ramona was surprised because the doctor was ________.

a. wearing glasses
b. young
c. late
d. tall

4. At first, the doctor felt ________ about Lourdes.

a. good
b. worried
c. bad
d. upset

C Answer the questions.

1. Ramona is 55 years old. How old is Isabel? Isabel is ______________ ______________ ______________.
2. What does Isabel do? She is a ______________.
3. Why did Doctor Valenzuela ask for the nurse? ______________
____

Work with the Words

A Circle the correct answer.

1. My boss told me to do the work **immediately** because ________.
   a. the work was very important
   b. I was busy
   c. business was very slow
   d. we had a lot of time to do the work
2. I don't like to visit zoos because I am **afraid** of ________.
   a. children
   b. animals
   c. weather
   d. tickets
3. Mr. Martin was very **responsible** at work, so the company ________.
   a. fired him
   b. gave him more money
   c. took away his vacation time
   d. didn't like him
4. After Sylvia **recovered** from her operation, she felt ________.
   a. terrible
   b. sick
   c. good
   d. tired
5. The children were **awake** because they were ________.
   a. sleepy
   b. tired
   c. bored
   d. excited
6. Ms. Smith has to **rush** because she ________.
   a. likes to be late
   b. isn't worried about the time
   c. has a lot of time
   d. is late for an appointment

7. He's sad because he **misses** ________.
   a. the bus
   b. the doctor
   c. his family
   d. the exam

8. My grandmother had her operation in the ________ department of the hospital.
   a. visiting
   b. nurse's
   c. surgical
   d. emergency

9. After school is over, ________ are going to **pick up** their children.
   a. the parents
   b. the teachers
   c. the classes
   d. the principal

B Complete the sentences with the correct words and phrases.

afraid	**immediately**	**miss**	**recover**	**rush**
awake	**looks like**	**pick me up**	**responsible**	

1. My supervisor asked me to help because she thinks that I am ______________.
2. I am ______________ of small spaces, so I don't like to ride the elevator.
3. My father died 10 years ago, but I still ______________ him.
4. Can you ______________ today? It's raining hard.
5. Veronica ______________ her sister, Vanessa, so everyone knows they are sisters.
6. Turn off the oven ______________ or the food will burn.
7. Mr. Rose is going to ______________ quickly from his surgery because he is in good health.
8. (*Mother to teenager*) It's late. Why are you ______________? Go to bed.
9. Ed is going to ______________ to work because his boss told him not to be late again.

C Answer the questions.

1. Who **picked** Ramona **up** at the airport? _______________
2. Who **looks like** Ramona? _______________
3. Who did Ramona **miss**? _______________
4. Why did Ramona and Isabel **rush** to the hospital? _______________
5. Why did Ramona and her sister **whisper** in their mother's hospital room? _______________
6. Why do you think Ramona is **afraid** in the hospital?

   ____
7. Is Lourdes **recovering** quickly? _______________
8. Was Lourdes **awake** when Doctor Valenzuela was in her room?

   ____

Lifeskill Practice

Hospital vocabulary

Complete the sentences with the correct words and phrases.

chart	**recover**	**surgical nurse**
reception desk	**stroke**	**visiting hours**

1. A family can see hospital patients during _______________.
2. The doctor can read about a patient on the patient's

   _______________.
3. A _______________ works in the operating room.
4. You can get information about a patient at the _______________.
5. A _______________ is an injury to the brain.
6. The opposite of *get worse* is _______________.

Dialogue Practice

Practice the conversation with three classmates.

Ramona: Mami? Are you awake?

Lourdes: I was trying to sleep, but you girls are talking too much. Ramona? Is that you? What are you doing here?

Ramona: Isabel called me yesterday, and I arrived 30 minutes ago. How do you feel?

Lourdes: A little better, but tired. Ramona, what about the flower shop? Who's taking care of the business?"

Ramona: Don't worry, Mami. Nelly is taking care of everything. I'm going to stay here for a while. I want to talk to the doctor. What's his name?

Isabel: Ramona, relax. Everything is fine. We have a good doctor. Doctor Valenzuela is a friend of the family. We have an appointment with him tomorrow morning at 8:30. He'll meet us here.

Nina: I'm sorry, but your mother needs rest. We'll take good care of her.

Ramona: All right. I'll see you tomorrow, Mami.

Lourdes: See you tomorrow, Ramona. You, too, Isabel.

Isabel: Good night, Mami. Thanks, Nina. My sister feels much better now.

Nina: You're welcome.

A Quick Recovery

Get Ready to Read

A Discuss with a partner.

1. Why are Ramona and Isabel upset?
2. How is their mother?
3. What do you think the doctor is going to say to them?

B Match the words and expressions with the definitions.

_d_	1. calm	a.	new, recently picked from a garden
____	2. familiar	b.	thinking in a positive way
____	3. fresh	c.	afraid
____	4. improve	d.	peaceful, relaxed
____	5. optimistic	e.	felt good after something bad did not happen
____	6. relieved	f.	something that you know: a voice, a face, a place
____	7. scared	g.	get better

In the last episode...

Ramona arrived in Manzanillo, Mexico, at about eleven o'clock last night. She and her sister, Isabel, went directly to the hospital to see their mother, Lourdes. At the hospital, Isabel talked to the head nurse, Nina. Nina said that visiting hours were over, but she let them go visit for a short time. Ramona and Isabel talked to their mother for a few minutes.

The next day, they talked to Dr. Valenzuela, their mother's doctor. Everyone was very **optimistic**. Suddenly, something happened and a machine began to beep. The doctor told them to leave the room.

“Mami, Mami! Doctor, what’s happening?” asks Isabel.

Dr. Valenzuela goes to the other side of the bed. He’s looking at the machines. “Get the nurse!” he shouts to Isabel.

A nurse runs into the room. “What is it?”

“Call Dr. Zamora.”

“What’s going on?” asks Isabel. Ramona is too worried to speak.

Dr. Valenzuela looks at the sisters and says, “Please wait outside. I’ll come talk to you later.”

Ramona and Isabel leave the room. At first, they look through the window into their mother’s room. There are two nurses in the room now, and another doctor, Dr. Zamora, rushes into the room. He is speaking to Dr. Valenzuela. Then one of the nurses closes the **blinds,**[*] and the sisters can’t see into the room. They go into the waiting area across from the room. Ramona is very upset, but Isabel is a nurse and works in the same hospital. She knows that Dr. Valenzuela and Dr. Zamora are excellent doctors, so she is **calm.**

“Calm down, Ramona. Mami’s strong. She’ll be OK. I’m sure,” says Isabel.

“I’m **scared**, Isabel.”

“I know you are. I am, too, but the doctors here are very good.”

A half-hour passes, and then a nurse comes to talk to the sisters. “The doctor says that your mother is **stable**[**] for now.”

“What happened?” asks Isabel.

“The doctor will explain everything in a little while. Why don’t you go to the cafeteria and get some coffee?”

Isabel gets up. “Come on, Ramona. Let’s go to the cafeteria and get some coffee. I’ll talk to the nurse at the desk and tell her where we’re going. I have my cell phone. If anything happens, they’ll contact us.”

Ramona stands up. “OK, but I want to go to the chapel first.”

Ramona and Isabel talk to the nurse at the desk. She promises to call them when the doctors are free to talk to them. First, Ramona and Isabel take the elevator to the ground floor to visit the chapel. Then they go to the cafeteria for some coffee. At about ten o’clock, Isabel’s cell phone rings. The sisters run to the elevator, but they can’t wait. They take the stairs and run up to the fourth floor,

[*]**blinds** = window coverings, usually made of plastic or wood

[**]**stable** = stays the same

the intensive care floor. When they get to their mother's room, they see Dr. Valenzuela and Dr. Zamora talking to a nurse.

Dr. Valenzuela introduces Dr. Zamora to Ramona. "This is Mrs. Rivera, and I think you know her sister, Isabel Molina. She's a surgical nurse here." Dr. Zamora shakes their hands and says, "Nice to meet you. You can go in to see your mother, but just for a few minutes. She's awake now, but she needs her rest."

"What happened?" asks Isabel.

"Your mother had a bad reaction to one of the medications. We changed it, and now she's **improving** quickly. We'll watch her carefully."

"Thank you so much," says Isabel, and she and Ramona rush into their mother's room. Lourdes is a little weak, but she's smiling at her daughters.

"How are you feeling, Mami? We were so worried," says Ramona.

"Much better. You two look terrible."

Both Ramona and Isabel laugh. They are very happy to hear their mother's voice, and they feel very **relieved**.

* * * *

Ramona is still in Manzanillo two weeks later. It's a friendly town. Ramona lived here until she was five, and she is happy to be back in the town where she was born. She's also happy to be with her mother and sister again. They have a small but nice house in Manzanillo. There are some tourists in the town, but it's not crowded like Acapulco or Cancun. Isabel likes it because all the neighbors are friendly, and she can walk to work at the hospital in a few minutes. Life is slower here. People are more relaxed. Ramona likes to visit her family here, and she knows many of the neighbors because she tries to visit three or four times a year.

Lourdes is out of intensive care. In fact, she's coming home tomorrow, so Ramona is at the market. She wants to prepare a special dinner for her mother. The markets in Mexico are wonderful. There are many **fresh** fruits and vegetables, and they're cheap.

Ramona is **picking out**[*] some mangoes. She is putting the mangoes in her shopping bag. Suddenly, she hears a **familiar** voice.

"Ramona? Is that you?"

Ramona looks up. She sees a tall, handsome man with **salt-and-pepper hair**[**] and a mustache. "Vicente? Is that really you? I can't believe it! What are you doing here?"

[*]**pick out** = choose

[**]**salt-and-pepper hair** = hair that is partly gray, partly black

Reading Comprehension

A Circle *True* or *False.*

1. Ramona and Isabel slept in their mother's room. **True** **False**
2. The nurse gave them all the information about their mother. **True** **False**
3. Isabel saw the doctors right away. **True** **False**
4. Ramona is scared when she gets to the hospital. **True** **False**
5. The nurse gives them a cell phone. **True** **False**
6. When the cell phone rings, they are in the cafeteria. **True** **False**
7. Lourdes had a reaction to the flowers in her room. **True** **False**
8. Later, Lourdes is weak but better. **True** **False**

B Circle the correct answer.

1. When did Ramona arrive in Mexico?
   - **a.** two days ago
   - **b.** two months ago
   - **c.** two weeks ago
   - **d.** two hours ago
2. Isabel likes Manzanillo because ________.
   - **a.** it's very crowded with tourists
   - **b.** there is nothing to do
   - **c.** she doesn't know the neighbors
   - **d.** life is slower and the neighbors are friendly
3. How does Isabel get to work?
   - **a.** She drives.
   - **b.** She walks.
   - **c.** She takes a bus.
   - **d.** She takes a subway.
4. Ramona is preparing a special meal because ________.
   - **a.** her mother is coming home
   - **b.** she is getting ready to go back to New Jersey
   - **c.** Vicente is coming to dinner
   - **d.** she wants to thank the nurses

C **Put the sentences in order from 1 to 8.**

_____ The cell phone rings.

_____ Dr. Valenzuela calls for another doctor.

_____ Ramona and Isabel go to the hospital chapel.

__1__ Lourdes has a bad reaction to medicine.

_____ Ramona meets an old friend.

_____ Ramona and Isabel go to the cafeteria.

_____ Dr. Zamora enters Lourdes's room.

_____ Isabel and Ramona talk to the nurse at the desk.

Work with the Words

A **Match the words with their opposites.**

_____ **1.** calm

_____ **2.** familiar

_____ **3.** fresh

_____ **4.** improve

_____ **5.** optimistic

_____ **6.** relieved

_____ **7.** scared

a. upset; worried

b. old

c. strange; something that you don't know

d. not afraid

e. get worse

f. felt bad after something happened

g. become upset; excited

B **Circle the correct answer.**

1. Please close the ________. The sun is too strong in here.

a. door
b. blinds
c. window
d. air conditioner

2. After the exam, the student was **relieved** because ________.

a. the test wasn't hard
b. he had another test later
c. he fell asleep
d. the test was very difficult

3. My English **improved** after ________.
   a. I continued to speak my first language
   b. I didn't take a class
   c. I started listening to English radio programs
   d. I stopped studying English
4. The doctor was **optimistic** because the operation was ________.
   a. successful
   b. not successful
   c. full of problems
   d. long
5. That woman looks **familiar**. I think ________.
   a. I never saw her
   b. she is new here
   c. I know her
   d. I don't know her
6. **Fresh** food usually tastes ________.
   a. hot
   b. very good
   c. bad
   d. old
7. I was **scared** the first time that I ________.
   a. was on time for my class
   b. went to the movies
   c. had a birthday party
   d. went on an airplane
8. My children's doctor is very **calm**, so my children are ________.
   a. not nervous
   b. afraid
   c. nervous
   d. worried

C Who does the sentence describe? You may use some names more than once.

Dr. Valenzuela	**Isabel**	**Ramona**	**Vicente**
Dr. Zamora	**Lourdes**	**The desk nurse**	

1. ____________________ is **optimistic**.
2. ____________________ is **calm**.
3. ____________________ is **scared**.
4. ____________________ is **familiar** to Ramona.
5. ____________________ is **improving**.
6. ____________________ and ____________________ are **relieved**.

Lifeskill Practice

■ **How do you get to work? How long does it take?**

A **Practice the conversations with a classmate.**

1. **A:** How do you get to work?
   B: I take the bus.

   A: How long does it take?
   B: It takes about 20 minutes.

2. **A:** How does she get to work?
   B: She drives.

   A: How long does it take?
   B: It takes about 30 minutes.

B **Complete the conversation with your own information.**

A: How do you get to school?
B: I ____________________.
A: How long does it take?
B: It takes ____________________.

C **Practice your conversation with a classmate.**

Dialogue Practice

Practice the conversation with two classmates.

Isabel: Calm down, Ramona. Mami's strong. She'll be OK. I'm sure.
Ramona: I'm scared, Isabel.
Isabel: I know you are. I am, too, but the doctors here are very good.
Nurse: The doctor says that your mother is stable for now.
Isabel: What happened?
Nurse: The doctor will explain everything in a little while. Why don't you go to the cafeteria and get some coffee?

Isabel: Come on, Ramona. Let's go to the cafeteria and get some coffee. I'll talk to the nurse at the desk and tell her where we're going. I have my cell phone. If anything happens, they will contact us.

Ramona: OK, but I want to go to the chapel first.

Practice the conversation with four classmates.

Dr. Valenzuela: This is Mrs. Rivera, and I think you know her sister, Isabel Molina. She's a surgical nurse here.

Dr. Zamora: Nice to meet you. You can go in to see your mother, but just for a few minutes. She's awake now, but she needs her rest.

Isabel: What happened?

Dr. Zamora: Your mother had a bad reaction to one of the medications. We changed it, and now she's improving quickly. We'll watch her carefully.

Isabel: Thank you so much.

Ramona: How are you feeling, Mami? We were so worried.

Lourdes: Much better. You two look terrible.

An Old Friend

Get Ready to Read

A **Discuss with a partner.**

1. Why is Ramona at the market?
2. Who is the man next to Ramona?
3. What do you think is going to happen next?

B **Match the words and expressions with the definitions.**

__c__ **1.** drop
____ **2.** depend (on)
____ **3.** pay attention (to)
____ **4.** healthy (food)
____ **5.** interrupt
____ **6.** know how to
____ **7.** habits

a. things that you do every day without thinking
b. stop someone's conversation, usually by talking
c. allow something to fall, usually to the floor
d. watch; be careful
e. influenced by something or someone
f. good for your body
g. can do something

In the last episode...

Ramona and Isabel were very worried about their mother. She had a bad reaction to a medication, and Ramona was very scared. Dr. Valenzuela called for another doctor, Dr. Zamora. Ramona and Isabel had to leave their mother's hospital room for a short time, so they went to the hospital chapel. After that, they went to the cafeteria. Later, the desk nurse called them, and they returned to their mother's room. She was better, and Ramona and Isabel had a chance to talk to the doctors and to their mother. Everyone was relieved.

It's two weeks later, and Ramona's mother, Lourdes, is coming home from the hospital. Ramona wants to prepare a special meal for her, so she's buying some fresh fruit from the market. She also finds some large avocados. She puts the mangoes and avocados into her shopping bag. Suddenly, she hears a familiar voice.

"Ramona? Is that you?"

A tall, handsome man is standing behind Ramona. Ramona looks up. The man is smiling. He has salt-and-pepper hair and a moustache.

"Vicente? Vicente Fuentes? Is it really you? What are you doing here?" Ramona **drops** her shopping bag on the ground. The mangoes and the avocados fall on the ground.

Vicente smiles and says, "Let me help you, Ramona."

Ramona looks down. She's smiling and laughing, too. "I thought your face was familiar. I was so surprised to see you. I wasn't **paying attention**." Ramona and Vicente put the mangoes and avocados back into her shopping bag, and she starts to pay for the fruit. Vicente is holding the shopping bag.

"So, Vicente, what are you doing here? Why aren't you in Texas?"

"I'll ask the same question. Why aren't you in New Jersey?"

"Well, my mother had a stroke, Vicente. She's in the hospital, and . . . "

Vicente **interrupts.** "In the hospital? I'm so sorry, Ramona. How is she doing? Is it serious?"

Ramona smiles and answers, "We have good news. She's coming home today. That's why I'm at the market. I want to prepare a special dinner for her. In fact, I really have to go. It's 10:30 and I have to go home. Isabel and I are going to pick up Mami. The doctor is going to **discharge*** her today. It was really nice to see you again. Maybe I'll see you again before I go back to New Jersey."

"Back to New Jersey?" Vicente looks disappointed. "When are you going back?"

"I'm not sure yet. It **depends on** my mother's health. I really have to go now. It was nice to see you. Bye!"

Ramona walks away. She turns around and **waves.**** Vicente is standing in front of the market. He smiles and waves. Then he thinks to himself, "Ramona Rivera. What a surprise to see her again."

***discharge** (someone) = give someone permission to leave the hospital

****wave** = to move your hand from side to side to say *hello* or *good-bye*

* * * *

It is late morning, and Ramona and Isabel are filling out forms at the front desk of the hospital. Lourdes is waiting for Dr. Valenzuela to **discharge** her.

"Good morning, Mrs. Cruz."

"Good morning, Dr. Valenzuela. Can I go home now?"

"Just a minute. We have to sign a few papers, and then you can go home. First, I would like to introduce you to someone. This is Ms. Lima."

A tall, attractive woman in a suit walks into the room. She walks to Lourdes and shakes her hand. "Nice to meet you, Mrs. Cruz."

Dr. Valenzuela says, "Isabel, Ramona, I'd like to introduce you to Ms. Lima. Ms. Lima, these are Mrs. Cruz's daughters, Isabel Molina and Ramona Rivera."

Dr. Valenzuela continues, "Ms. Lima is a **nutritionist**.* She's going to talk to you about changing your eating **habits**."

Dr. Valenzuela turns to Lourdes. "After you finish with Ms. Lima, you can go home. I'll see you in my office next week."

"Thank you, Doctor," says Lourdes.

Ms. Lima says, "Now, as Dr. Valenzuela said, I'm here to talk about your eating habits. Mrs. Cruz, you are in good shape for your age. I understand that you walk to the market every day, and you volunteer at the elementary school a couple of times a week. Is that right?"

"Yes, that's right," answers Lourdes.

"But, your **cholesterol**** is too high. You have to stop eating so much oil, sugar, and fatty foods."

***nutritionist** = an expert who knows about healthy food and vitamins

****cholesterol** = an unhealthy chemical in fat and blood

"I'm sure we all need to eat more **healthy** food," says Isabel.

Ms. Lima opens a folder and pulls out a couple of papers. "Here is a list of foods that your mother can eat often, foods that she can eat once in a while, and foods she should stay away from. I'm giving you some recipes, too. They're pretty good, and they're healthy."

Lourdes looks at the list. "It's time to make some changes. Two weeks in the hospital is enough."

Ms. Lima gives everyone her business cards. She says, "Here is my office telephone number. Please feel free to call me if you have any questions."

Ramona thanks the nutritionist, and Ms. Lima leaves. "Well, let's go home."

* * * *

It's 5:30. Lourdes is sitting on the patio of her house. It's a warm spring evening. She is sitting in the sun. Isabel comes out to the patio. She smiles.

"How are you feeling, Mami?"

"I feel fine. It's good to be in my own house. I hate hospitals. Those nurses woke me up at six o'clock in the morning and turned the lights out at nine o'clock at night. I'm happy to be home. Mmmm. What's that wonderful smell?"

"Ramona is cooking all of your favorites, but without the oil and the fat. Are you hungry?"

"When are we going to eat?"

The patio is outside of the kitchen. Ramona looks out the window.

"Dinner's ready! Do you want to eat on the patio? It's a nice evening."

"That's a wonderful idea, Ramona."

"I'll set the table," says Isabel. "Mami, what do you want to drink?"

"I'll have soda, please," answers Lourdes.

"No soda," says Ramona from the kitchen. "Soda is not on the list."

"OK. I'll have water," says Lourdes.

It's quiet on the patio. There's a blue and yellow tablecloth on the table. Two candles are in the middle of the table. It's full of typical Mexican dishes. Ramona, Isabel, and Lourdes are sitting around the table. No one's talking. They're enjoying the food. Isabel looks at her mother's empty soup bowl.

"Ramona, do you think Mami is a little hungry?" Isabel asks, smiling.

Lourdes says, "Oh, be quiet. Hospital food is terrible. Ramona, you're an excellent cook. This tastes good. Are you sure that you didn't use oil?"

"I'm sure," says Ramona, "I followed Ms. Lima's instructions. And I **know how to** cook because I had a great teacher." Lourdes is an excellent cook, too. She taught Ramona and Isabel how to cook.

"Oh, I forget to tell you some news," says Ramona. "Guess who I saw in the market today? Vicente Fuentes."

Isabel drops her fork on the table. "Vicente Fuentes? You're kidding! Is he still handsome?"

"Who's Vicente Fuentes?" asks Lourdes.

"Don't you remember, Mami?" says Isabel. "He was Ramona's boyfriend in high school."

"Oh, I remember him. He was a very handsome young man from a good family. He was an excellent student, too. Why didn't you marry him, Ramona?"

Lourdes continues eating her dinner. Ramona looks at her mother. She's surprised at what she's saying.

The telephone rings. Isabel runs to answer it. She yells from the kitchen, "Ramona, it's for you!"

Reading Comprehension

A Circle *True* or *False.*

1. Ramona's mother is coming home today. **True** **False**
2. Vicente is a short, unattractive man. **True** **False**
3. Ramona was surprised to see her old friend. **True** **False**
4. Ramona and Vicente go out to dinner to talk. **True** **False**
5. Isabel goes by herself to pick up Lourdes. **True** **False**
6. Lourdes has high cholesterol. **True** **False**
7. The nutritionist gave Lourdes a food list. **True** **False**
8. Lourdes will continue to have oil and fat in her food. **True** **False**

B Circle the correct answer.

1. Lourdes didn't like ________ at the hospital.
   a. the beds **c.** the people
   b. the food **d.** the doctors
2. Who is cooking dinner?
   a. Isabel **c.** Ramona
   b. Lourdes **d.** a cook
3. The patio is ________ the kitchen.
   a. far from **c.** in
   b. above **d.** outside of
4. What does Lourdes remember about Vicente?
   a. He was handsome. **c.** He was from a good family.
   b. He was not a good student. **d.** Both a and c.

C **Complete the information about Vicente Fuentes.**

Vicente Fuentes is tall and ________________. He has ________________-and-________________ hair and a ________________. Vicente is from a ________________ family. He was a/an ________________ ________________ in high school. He was Ramona's ________________ when they were in high school.

D **Who said it? Write the name of the person.**

Dr. Valenzuela	**Ms. Lima**	**Vicente**
Lourdes	**Ramona**	

1. ______________ "I want to prepare a special dinner for her."

2. ______________ "How is she doing? Is it serious?"

3. ______________ "We have to sign a few papers, and then you can go home."

4. ______________ "Two weeks in the hospital is enough."

5. ______________ "No soda. Soda is not on the list."

6. ______________ "I'll see you in my office next week."

7. ______________ "You eat too much oil, too much sugar, and too much fat."

8. ______________ "Why didn't you marry him?"

Work with the Words

A **Circle the correct answer.**

1. We want to have a picnic on Saturday, but it **depends on** ________.
   - **a.** the weather
   - **b.** the rain
   - **c.** the food
   - **d.** the price

2. He got the job because he **knows how to** ________.
   - **a.** have a good time
   - **b.** walk
   - **c.** take a vacation
   - **d.** use a computer

3. Which is a **healthy** lunch?
   a. tuna fish with lots of mayonnaise, two bowls of rice, and a soda
   b. two hot dogs and a bottle of water
   c. a hamburger with French fries and a soda
   d. a turkey sandwich on whole grain bread and unsweetened iced tea
4. When you drive, you must **pay attention to** ________.
   a. the radio
   b. the traffic
   c. your clothes
   d. your cell phone
5. I don't want the phone to **interrupt** me at work. Please ________.
   a. call me after work
   b. call me at work
   c. turn up the phone
   d. don't call me at home
6. If you **drop** a glass, ________.
   a. it will break
   b. it will get dirty
   c. you can drink from it
   d. it will be wet
7. A **nutritionist** can tell you ________.
   a. about healthy food
   b. about fast food and where to buy it
   c. how to cook fast food
   d. where the gym is
8. She has some good **habits**:
   a. She sleeps four hours a night.
   b. She exercises five times a week.
   c. She drives everywhere.
   d. She always eats a big meal before bed.
9. The baby was so happy to see us! He was smiling and ________.
   a. sleeping
   b. crying
   c. sitting
   d. waving

B **Complete the sentences with the correct words and phrases. You do not need all the words.**

depends on	**drop**	**healthy**	**nutritionist**	**waving**
discharge	**habits**	**interrupt**	**pays attention to**	

1. My mother always said that children shouldn't ______________.
2. The ______________ told me not to eat cake and cookies.
3. Someone is ______________ to me from across the street. His face looks familiar, but I can't remember his name.
4. The doctor always ______________ his patients' blood pressure and cholesterol.
5. Be careful. Don't ______________ your camera! You don't want it to break.
6. The doctor is going to ______________ his patient from the hospital this afternoon.
7. I'd like to have an outdoor wedding, but it ______________ the weather.
8. My father needs to change his eating ______________. He loves salt and fat!

C **Answer the questions.**

1. What does Ramona do when she says good-bye to Vicente at the market? ______________________________
2. How long is Ramona going to stay in Manzanillo?
   It depends on ______________________________
3. Why did Ramona **drop** the fruit?
   She wasn't ______________________________
4. Who **interrupted** Ramona while she was talking?
   ____
5. Who **discharged** Lourdes from the hospital?
   ____
6. What is Ms. Lima's job?
   ____
7. Who is going to change her eating **habits**?
   ____

Lifeskill Practice

Use *know how to*

Ramona says, "I **know how to** cook because I had a great teacher."

A Circle the answers that are true about yourself.

1. I **know how to / don't know** how to cook.
2. I **know how to / don't know** how to speak French.
3. I **know how to / don't know** how to get to the airport.
4. I **know how to / don't know** how to swim.
5. I **know how to / don't know** how to take care of children.

B Practice the conversations with a classmate.

1. **A:** Do you **know how to** cook?
   B: Yes, I do.
2. **B:** Do you **know how to** cook?
   A: No, I don't, but I can learn.

C Practice the conversations in Part B with the phrases in the box. Give true answers about yourself.

answer the phone	**fix a copy machine**
dance salsa	**use a cash register**
fix a car	**use a computer**

Dialogue Practice

Practice the conversation with two classmates.

Isabel: Ramona, do you think Mami is a little hungry?

Lourdes: Oh, be quiet. Hospital food is terrible. Ramona, you're an excellent cook. This tastes good. Are you sure you didn't use oil?

Ramona: Thanks, Mother, but I had a very good teacher. I'm sure. I followed Ms. Lima's instructions. And I know how to cook because I had a great teacher. Oh, I forget to tell you some news. Guess who I saw in the market today? Vicente Fuentes.

Isabel: Vicente Fuentes? You're kidding! Is he still handsome?

Lourdes: Who's Vicente Fuentes?

Isabel: Don't you remember, Mami? He was Ramona's boyfriend in high school.

Lourdes: Oh, I remember him. He was a very handsome young man from a good family. He was an excellent student, too. Why didn't you marry him, Ramona?

(*The telephone rings.*)

Isabel: Ramona, it's for you!

A Long Cup of Coffee

Get Ready to Read

A **Discuss with a partner.**

1. When did Lourdes come home from the hospital?
2. What are Ramona, Isabel, and Lourdes eating and drinking?
3. Who is on the telephone?

B **Match the words and phrases with the definitions.**

_d_	**1.** run into	**a.** an appointment to meet someone; usually romantic
____	**2.** just	**b.** like better
____	**3.** bother	**c.** a few minutes ago
____	**4.** overhear	**d.** to meet someone by chance
____	**5.** change the subject	**e.** annoy; interrupt
____	**6.** prefer	**f.** hear someone else's conversation, usually by accident
____	**7.** date	**g.** talk about something new

In the last episode...

Ramona was at the market when she saw an old friend, Vicente Fuentes. She was happy to see him, but she didn't have time to stay and talk because she had to go to the hospital to pick up her mother. Vicente was disappointed.

At the hospital, Dr. Valenzuela discharged Lourdes, but first he introduced her to a nutritionist, Ms. Lima. Ms. Lima talked to Lourdes and her daughters about healthy eating habits. She gave them a food list and some recipes. Now Ramona, Isabel, and Lourdes are at home. Ramona cooked a nice, healthy meal for everyone. During dinner, Ramona tells her mother and sister about Vicente Fuentes, who was an old boyfriend. Then the telephone rings. It's a call for Ramona.

Ramona goes to the kitchen to answer the telephone. Isabel is standing in the kitchen with. a big smile on her face. Ramona looks at Isabel. She is waiting for Isabel to go back outside, but Isabel doesn't move.

"Isabel, I think Mami's calling for you," she says with a **frown.***

"OK, OK. I'll leave, but I want to know everything as soon as you finish talking!" Isabel goes back outside to finish her dinner.

"Hello?" answers Ramona.

"Hello, Ramona. This is Vicente Fuentes. Uh . . . how's your mother doing?"

"Oh, thank you for asking, Vicente. She's doing fine. She's happy to be back home, and she definitely **prefers** to have a home-cooked meal. We're eating dinner right now on the patio."

"Oh, I'm sorry. You're eating dinner. I'm **bothering** you."

"That's OK, Vicente. How did you get my phone number?"

"Well, uh . . . I know one of your sister's friends from the hospital and I asked her. Ramona, you said that you were going back to New Jersey. I know you're very busy, and your mother **just** got home from the hospital, but I'd like to see

*__frown__ = sad or angry face; opposite of *smile*

you again. We can talk about old times. Would you like to meet me for coffee tonight?"

"Meet you tonight?" asks Ramona. "I don't know, Vicente. My mother just got home from the hospital. I think I **should*** stay home tonight."

"Isn't your sister there with your mother?" asks Vicente.

"Yes, that's true, but I think I should stay home. I can't go out. This is my mother's first night home."

Isabel and Lourdes are standing at the kitchen door. They **overhear** part of Ramona's conversation. They're whispering to Ramona, "Go ahead. We'll be fine! Go on! Go out!"

"Well, Ramona," Vicente says in a disappointed voice, "maybe we can meet another time."

"Well . . . actually, Vicente, you know . . . well, my sister is living here, and she took the day off to stay home with our mother. No, tonight is fine. What time would you like to meet?"

* * * *

It's 9:30 in the evening, and Vicente and Ramona are sitting at a café in the center of town. They arrived at the café at nine o'clock. At first, Ramona was quiet, but now she's very talkative. Vicente is smiling a lot. Ramona and Vicente are talking about the past 25 years. Ramona's having a good time. She thinks to herself, "Vicente looks good after all these years."

*I **should** stay at home = *I think it is better if I stay at home*

"So, Vicente, I told you everything about my family. What about you?"

"Well, you remember my wife, Rosita."

Ramona's face changes. She looks a little upset, but then she smiles again.

"Yes, I remember her. How is she?"

"Well, I guess she's OK. Rosita left me for another man a year after we got married. Our daughter was a baby."

"What? No! I can't believe it. Rosita left you? What about your daughter? Did she take her away?"

"No, she didn't. She left our daughter with me. As you know, we were very young. I didn't know how to take care of a baby. Fortunately, my mother helped me a lot. Would you like to see a picture?"

Vicente gets his wallet and pulls out a picture of a young woman.

"This is Lupe."

Ramona looks at the picture. "She's beautiful, Vicente. I see that she has Rosita's eyes."

"Yes, she does. Let's **change the subject**. What was I talking about? Oh, I went to the university and finished my business degree. After I graduated, I got a job with my father's company. I travel between the States and Mexico very often. I was tired of staying in hotels, so I just bought a new house near here. Would you like to see it? It's very nice."

"It's getting late, Vicente. I have to go."

"OK. Maybe another time."

Vicente walks Ramona to her mother's house. "Good night, Vicente. It was nice to see you again."

"Good night, Ramona. Can I see you again tomorrow?"

"Maybe, if I'm not too busy." Ramona goes inside the house.

* * * *

Since that first evening at the café last week, Ramona and Vicente have met every night. They go for a walk, go to the café, and just talk. Now it's eight o'clock one week later, and Ramona is getting dressed for another **date** with Vicente. Lourdes is in the bedroom watching her. Lourdes is feeling much better. Every morning Ramona and her mother take a walk to the plaza in the center of town and they sit and watch the people. Ramona's enjoying the time with her mother. She's very relieved that her mother's feeling better.

"Ramona," says her mother. "You've been here for three weeks. I'm feeling much better now. When are you going to go back to New Jersey? What about your business?"

"Everything is fine back home, Mami. Nelly is watching the store. My tenant and Margarita are taking care of Mambo. I think I'll stay a little longer."

"Are you staying because of me, or are you staying because of Vicente?"

At that moment, Ramona's cell phone rings. Ramona quickly answers the phone. "Hello?"

"Mom, when are you coming home?" It is Margarita, Ramona's daughter, calling from New Jersey.

"Margarita! How are you? Is anything wrong?" asks Ramona.

"Nothing's wrong. You didn't call yesterday. I was worried," says Margarita. "How's Grandma?"

"Grandma's fine, honey," says Ramona. "Listen, I'll call you tomorrow. I have an appointment. I have to go. Here, Mami. Talk to your granddaughter." Ramona gives the telephone to her mother.

Margarita is confused. She's thinking, "What's going on? An appointment? At night? What kind of appointment does she have?"

"Hello, Margarita. How's my favorite granddaughter?" says Lourdes.

Margarita answers, "Grandma, I'm glad that you're feeling better. Where's Mom going?"

Lourdes smiles and says, "Margarita, your mother has a date."

"A date! With who?"

"With her old boyfriend, Vicente. She **ran into** him at the market last week."

Margarita is shocked. Her mother never goes out with anyone except her friends at the shop. Who is she meeting? "Grandma, I'll call back tomorrow. I have to go now. Love you. Bye!"

A few minutes later, Margarita is talking to her brother, Ernesto. He's a television cameraman. He lives in Los Angeles, California.

"Hello?"

"Ernesto, something's going on with Mom."

"What are you talking about, Rita? Is everything OK?"

"I want you to go to Manzanillo."

"Is Grandma OK? Is something wrong?" Ernesto is worried.

"No, Grandma Lourdes is doing much better. I spoke to her on the phone. The problem is Mom. She's been there for three weeks. When I called, she said she had an appointment, but Grandma said that she had a date!"

"A date! With who?"

"An old boyfriend. I can't go to Manzanillo right now because I just took my vacation. I can't take any more days off. Can you go there and find out what's going on? This is very unusual for Mom. I'm worried!"

"You're right. I'll leave tomorrow. I have to call the studio first to get a replacement. I'll take a few **personal days.*** I'll call you tomorrow night from Grandma's house."

***personal days** = days you can take off work to do things for yourself (not holidays)

Reading Comprehension

A Circle *True* or *False.*

1. Ramona calls Vicente on the telephone. **True** **False**
2. Isabel wants to hear Ramona's conversation. **True** **False**
3. Vicente asks about Ramona's mother. **True** **False**
4. Vicente is bothering Ramona and her family. **True** **False**
5. Vicente finds Ramona's telephone number in the phone book. **True** **False**
6. Vicente invites Ramona to have a cup of coffee. **True** **False**
7. Ramona is surprised to hear about Vicente's wife. **True** **False**
8. Ramona wants to visit Vicente's new house immediately. **True** **False**

B Circle the correct answer.

1. At first, Ramona doesn't want to go out with Vicente because ________.
   - **a.** her mother just came home
   - **b.** her sister doesn't like Vicente
   - **c.** she is worried about her mother
   - **d.** she doesn't like him
2. Lourdes thinks that Ramona ________.
   - **a.** is having a good time with Vicente
   - **b.** has a problem in New Jersey
   - **c.** should move to Mexico
   - **d.** both a and c
3. Ramona ________ goes out with men back in New Jersey.
   - **a.** sometimes
   - **b.** always
   - **c.** never
   - **d.** often
4. Margarita isn't going to Mexico because ________.
   - **a.** she doesn't like to fly
   - **b.** she doesn't have time off from work
   - **c.** she's going on vacation
   - **d.** she just came back from Mexico

C **Who does the sentence describe? You may use some names more than once.**

Ernesto **Isabel** **Lourdes** **Margarita** **Ramona** **Vicente**

1. ______________ just came home from the hospital.
2. ______________ is cooking a special meal.
3. ______________ and ______________ think that Ramona should go out with Vicente.
4. ______________ looks good after many years.
5. ______________ has a new house.
6. ______________ is worried about the florist shop in New Jersey.
7. ______________ lives in Los Angeles, California.
8. ______________ just took a vacation.
9. ______________ is going to Mexico tomorrow.

Work with the Words

A **Circle the correct answer.**

1. I am happy because I **ran into** ________ at the supermarket.
   a. a car
   b. an old friend
   c. some fresh vegetables
   d. some water
2. Where do couples go on **dates**?
   a. to an English class
   b. to work
   c. to a restaurant
   d. to the hospital
3. "Our son **just** graduated from high school" means ________.
   a. he graduated not long ago
   b. he graduated a few years ago
   c. he graduated a long time ago
   d. he is going to graduate tomorrow

4. When someone is **bothering** me, I feel ________.
   a. happy
   b. excited
   c. bored
   d. angry

5. It's late. The baby ________ go to sleep soon.
   a. doesn't have to
   b. won't
   c. should
   d. can't

6. What do you prefer: tennis or baseball?
   a. I am a good tennis player.
   b. tennis and baseball
   c. I don't like tennis.
   d. baseball

7. When I was in the hallway, I **overheard** ________.
   a. the television
   b. a conversation
   c. the radio
   d. the weather

8. My son always changes the subject when I ask about school. He ________.
   a. talks a lot
   b. doesn't talk a lot
   c. wants to talk about school
   d. doesn't want to talk about school

B **Complete the conversations with the correct words and phrases. You will not use all the words.**

bothering	**frowning**	**personal days**
change the subject	**just**	**prefer**
date	**overheard**	**ran into**

1. **A:** Excuse me. Am I ______________ you?
   B: No. May I help you?
2. **A:** Would you like soda or water?
   B: I ______________ water, thank you.
3. **A:** Why are you ______________?
   B: I just got my math score. It wasn't very good, and I'm angry!

4. **A:** Do you want to go to a movie?

   B: Don't ______________. We were talking about cleaning the house!

5. **A:** My son has the chicken pox. I have to stay home from work for a few days.

   B: You have five ______________. You can use them now.

6. **A:** Where are you going Friday night? Do you have a ______________?

   B: Yes, but my girlfriend has a cold. We're going to stay home and rent a movie.

7. **A:** How do you know about the layoffs? I didn't hear anything at the meeting.

   B: I was in the hallway. I ______________ the boss talking in the break room.

8. **A:** I saw your brother today.

   B: Really? Where?

   A: I ______________ him at the bookstore. Then we went out for coffee.

Lifeskill Practice

Use *Would you like to . . .*
Vicente says, "**Would you like to** meet me for coffee tonight?"
Would you like to is a polite way to make an invitation.

A **Practice the conversations.**

Vicente: Would you like to meet me for coffee tonight?
Ramona: I can't go out tonight. This is my mother's first night home.

A: Would you like to go to the movies?
B: Sure. What time should we meet?

A: Would you like to go to the party?
B: Yes, I would. Where's the party?

B Complete the invitations. Then practice the conversations with a classmate.

A: Would you like to ____________________?

B: Yes, I would. ____________________?

A: Would you like to ____________________?

B: Sure. ____________________?

Dialogue Practice

Practice the conversation with three classmates.

Ramona: Hello?

Vicente: Hello, Ramona. This is Vicente Fuentes. Uh . . . how's your mother doing?

Ramona: Oh, thank you for asking, Vicente. She's doing fine. She's happy to be back home, and she definitely prefers to have a home-cooked meal. We're eating dinner right now on the patio.

Vicente: Oh, I'm sorry. You're eating dinner. I'm bothering you.

Ramona: That's OK, Vicente. How did you get my phone number?

Vicente: Well, uh . . . I know one of your sister's friends from the hospital. I called her and asked her. Ramona, you said that you were going back to New Jersey. I know you're very busy, and your mother just got home from the hospital, but I'd like to see you again. We can talk about old times. Would you like to meet me for coffee tonight?

Ramona: Meet you tonight? I don't know, Vicente. My mother just got home from the hospital. I think I should stay at home tonight.

Vicente: Isn't your sister there with your mother?

Ramona: Yes, that's true, but I think I should stay home. I can't go out tonight. This is my mother's first night home.

Isabel and Lourdes: Go ahead. We will be fine! Go on! Go out!

Vicente: Well, Ramona. Maybe we can meet another time.

Ramona: Well . . . actually, Vicente, you know . . . well, my sister is living here, and she took the day off to stay home with our mother. No, tonight is fine. What time would you like to meet?

Who Is Vicente Fuentes?

Get Ready to Read

A **Discuss with a partner.**

1. Who is arriving in Mexico?
2. Is he going to meet Vicente?
3. What do you think Ernesto is going to do?

B **Match the words and expressions with the definitions.**

f	**1.** reluctant	**a.**	on another topic
____	**2.** find out	**b.**	end a relationship
____	**3.** by the way	**c.**	leave; stop attending (usually school)
____	**4.** break up	**d.**	feeling sad because you miss home, family, or friends
____	**5.** used to	**e.**	learn new information
____	**6.** homesick	**f.**	not want to do something
____	**7.** drop out (of)	**g.**	did (in the past, not now)

In the last episode...

Ramona was at home with her mother, Lourdes, and her sister, Isabel. They were eating dinner when the phone rang. It was Ramona's old boyfriend, Vicente Fuentes. He invited her out for coffee. At first Ramona was **reluctant** to go, but her mother and sister changed her mind. She had a nice evening with Vicente and **found out** that his wife, Rosita, left him many years ago after only one year of marriage. Ramona also learned that Vicente had a grown daughter. About a week later, Ramona's daughter, Margarita, called and was surprised to learn that her mother, who never went out with anyone in New Jersey, was out on a date with Vicente. She immediately called her brother, Ernesto, and asked him to go to Mexico to find out what was happening.

Ernesto arrives at the airport in Manzanillo and takes a taxi straight to his grandmother's house. Isabel and Lourdes are sitting in the kitchen. Isabel is making a nice lunch of tortillas and soup. Suddenly, they hear a knock at the door.

"Mami, watch the soup. I'll answer the door," says Isabel. She goes to the door and opens it.

"Ernesto!"

She gives him a big hug and a kiss. "What are you doing here? Come in! Come in!"

"Hi, Auntie Isabel! Where are Grandma Lourdes and Mom?" he asks.

"Grandma's in the kitchen. She'll be very happy to see you."

Isabel and Ernesto go into the kitchen. Lourdes is at the stove. She's stirring the soup. "What's for lunch?" asks Ernesto.

Lourdes stops stirring the soup and turns around. "Ernesto! My baby! My favorite grandson! Come here and give me a hug!" Lourdes and Ernesto hug and kiss each other warmly.

A few minutes later, Ernesto, Isabel, and Lourdes are sitting at the kitchen table. Ernesto is enjoying his lunch.

"Slow down, Ernesto! There's **plenty of*** soup," says Isabel.

"Sorry. I was **starving.**** The food on the airplane was terrible." Ernesto says with his mouth full of food.

"Leave him alone, Isabel," says Lourdes. "My grandson is hungry, and he hasn't eaten home-cooked food in a long time."

Ernesto kisses his grandmother on the cheek. "You know, Grandma, we were all very worried about you. Nando and Margarita send their love. You really look good."

"So, Ernesto," says Isabel, "what are you doing here?"

"Well, Margarita called me from New Jersey. She's worried about Mom. **By the way**, where is Mom?"

Lourdes smiles, "Your mother is out with a friend. So, Margarita was worried about Ramona's date."

*__plenty of__ = a lot of

**__starving__ = very hungry

“What do you mean ‘date’? I thought he was a friend. Tell me about him. She never goes out with anyone at home. Do you know the man?” asks Ernesto.

“She’s dating an old boyfriend named Vicente Fuentes,” says Isabel.

“What do you know about him?” asks Ernesto. “Is he nice? Does he have a good job?”

“You sound like your grandfather, Ernesto. Your mother is a grown woman. She can take care of herself.”

Isabel and Lourdes tell Ernesto everything they know about Vicente. Isabel starts, “Ernesto, you know that we **used to** live in Texas. Vicente and Ramona were high school sweethearts. His father was a businessman and owned an international food company. Your grandfather was a respected businessman, too, and he owned a large bookstore.

Both families were happy about your mother and Vicente. We thought that they would go to college, get engaged, and then get married. But something happened during their senior year in high school. Ramona and Vicente **broke up** for about four months. She was heartbroken and depressed.”

Lourdes adds, “Oh, she used to listen to sad music in her bedroom every day! Do you remember, Isabel?”

“I sure do,” says Isabel. “There were plenty of other young men who liked her, but she didn’t want to date anybody else. At the end of the school year, Ramona

and Vicente began dating again. Then, suddenly, they broke up again. Ramona never told us what happened. Immediately after graduation, Ramona went away to college, but she was very **homesick**, so she **dropped out** and came back home after the first semester. Then she started working at a florist. That's where she met your father. You know the rest of the story, Ernesto."

Ernesto asks, "Aunt Isabel, why did Mom and Vicente break up the second time?"

Isabel answers, "I don't know, Ernesto. Ask your mother."

"I don't understand," says Ernesto. "So, Mom sees Vicente every day? I want to meet him."

Isabel says, "You'll meet him tonight, Ernesto. He's coming for dinner with your mother."

* * * *

Later that evening, the front door opens. "I'm home! What's that delicious smell?" Ramona calls. "Where is everybody?"

"We're in the kitchen, Ramona," says Lourdes. "There's a surprise for you, too."

Ramona walks into the kitchen. Vicente Fuentes is walking behind her. "What surprise?"

Ernesto comes into the kitchen from the patio. "Hi, Mom!"

"Ernesto, what are you doing here? Are your brother and sister here, too?" Ramona hugs and kisses her son.

"No, Mom, they're back at home. It's just me," Ernesto says. He looks at Vicente.

Ramona looks at Ernesto, and then she looks at Vicente. "Oh, I'm sorry. Ernesto, this is Vicente Fuentes. Vicente, this is my youngest son, Ernesto. He's a cameraman in Los Angeles."

Ernesto and Vicente shake hands. "It's nice to meet you, Ernesto," says Vicente.

"Nice to meet you, too, Mr. Fuentes," says Ernesto.

"Please, don't be so formal. Call me Vicente."

"OK, Vicente. So, what did you two do today?"

"We're old friends, Ernesto. We were talking about old times," says Ramona. "Mami, Isabel, you remember Vicente, don't you?"

"Of course, I do," says Isabel. They kiss each other on the **cheeks**.*

Vicente looks at Lourdes. "Mrs. Cruz, you haven't changed in 20 years. You look wonderful. It's hard to believe that you were in the hospital." He gives her some flowers. "And these are for you, Isabel." Isabel thanks him and takes the flowers to put them in water.

"Thank you, Vicente. It's nice to see you again." Lourdes looks at everybody and says, "Let's eat. Dinner's ready."

Later, everyone is sitting on the patio waiting for coffee. Ramona is sitting between Ernesto and Vicente. Ernesto begins to ask Vicente a lot of questions. "So, Vicente, why are you in Manzanillo? Don't you live in Texas?"

*__cheeks__ = soft part of the face below the eyes

Reading Comprehension

A Circle *True* or *False.*

1. Ernesto called his aunt before his trip to Mexico. **True** **False**
2. Nando and Margarita sent presents for their grandmother. **True** **False**
3. Vicente and Ramona met in Texas. **True** **False**
4. Ramona was depressed after she broke up with Vicente. **True** **False**
5. Everyone knows why Ramona and Vicente broke up. **True** **False**
6. Ramona left college early. **True** **False**
7. Ramona met her husband at work. **True** **False**
8. Ernesto is happy to see Vicente. **True** **False**

B Circle the correct answer.

1. Ramona worked in ________.
   - **a.** a restaurant
   - **b.** her father's bookstore
   - **c.** a florist's shop
   - **d.** the college library
2. After high school, Ramona studied for ________.
   - **a.** one semester
   - **b.** one month
   - **c.** two semesters
   - **d.** more than a year
3. Ramona is ________ to see her son.
   - **a.** surprised
   - **b.** disappointed
   - **c.** upset
   - **d.** angry
4. After dinner, Ernesto ________.
   - **a.** is quiet
   - **b.** is angry at his mother
   - **c.** starts to ask Vicente a lot of questions
   - **d.** decides to go back to Los Angeles

C **Put the sentences in order from 1 to 7.**

____ Ramona left college and went back home.

__1__ Ramona and Vicente were high school sweethearts.

____ Ramona was depressed.

____ Ramona got a job and met Fernando Rivera.

____ Ramona became homesick.

____ Ramona went away to college.

____ Ramona and Vicente broke up.

Work with the Words

A **Circle the correct answer.**

1. I was **reluctant** to take the driving test because ________.
   a. I was ready to take it
   b. I didn't feel ready to take it
   c. I was an excellent driver
   d. I had a new car
2. How did you **find out** about your surprise party?
   a. I planned the party.
   b. I came home early and saw the cake.
   c. It was my birthday.
   d. It was a nice party.
3. Don and his girlfriend **broke up** because ________.
   a. he was too jealous
   b. she was a great girlfriend
   c. he was very nice to her
   d. his parents liked her a lot
4. The college student was very **homesick**, so she ________.
   a. did well on her assignments
   b. looked happy and excited
   c. made a lot of new friends
   d. called her parents twice a day
5. You don't need to bring a cake. We'll have **plenty of** ________ at the party.
   a. people
   b. desserts
   c. hamburgers
   d. soda

6. I didn't like any of my courses or professors, so I **dropped out of** ________.
   a. my books
   b. my room
   c. one course
   d. school

7. **A:** I'm really enjoying this movie.
   B: So am I. **By the way,** ________.
   a. I don't like action movies
   b. it's really good
   c. do you want to get something to drink?
   d. let's watch a movie

8. "We **used to** live in an apartment" means ________.
   a. "We live in an apartment now"
   b. "We like living in an apartment"
   c. "We don't live in an apartment now"
   d. "We are going to move into an apartment"

B Complete the sentences with the correct words and phrases.

broke up	**dropped out of**	**homesick**	**reluctant**	**used to**
by the way	**found out**	**plenty of**	**starving**	

1. Ernesto ____________ about his mother's boyfriend when he talked to his sister.
2. When Ramona started college, she was ____________, so she went back home.
3. Ramona was ____________ to tell her family about her relationship, so she didn't talk about it.
4. Did you know that Marissa's daughter ____________ college? It was too hard for her.
5. Ramona ____________ live in Texas. Now she lives in New Jersey.
6. There is always ____________ of food at Lourdes's home.
7. Ramona and Vicente ____________ before their graduation. No one knows what happened.
8. I didn't eat lunch, so I'm ____________! What's for dinner?
9. I ran into Bill at the market today, and he says hello. ____________, look at these beautiful strawberries they had today.

Lifeskill Practice

Introductions

A **Practice the conversation with two classmates.**

Ramona: Ernesto, this is Vicente Fuentes. Vicente, this is my son, Ernesto. He's a cameraman in Los Angeles.

Vicente: It's nice to meet you, Ernesto.

Ernesto: Nice to meet you, too, Mr. Fuentes.

Vicente: Please call me Vicente.

B **Work with two classmates. Complete the chart with information about them.**

	Classmate 1	Classmate 2
Occupation		
City		

C **Complete the conversation with the information in the chart from Exercise B. Use Exercise A as a model. Then practice the conversation together.**

You: ____________ (Classmate 2), this is ____________ (Classmate 1). ____________ (Classmate 1) is a ____________ (occupation) in ____________ (city).

Classmate 1: Nice to meet you, ____________ (Classmate 2).

Classmate 2: Nice to meet you too, Mr./Ms. ____________ (Classmate 1's last name).

Classmate 1: Please call me ____________ (Classmate 1's first name).

Dialogue Practice

Practice the conversation with two classmates.

(*A knock on the door*)

Isabel: Mami, watch the soup. I'll answer the door. (*She opens the door.*) Ernesto! What are you doing here? Come in! Come in!

Ernesto: Hi, Auntie Isabel! Where are Grandma Lourdes and Mom?

Isabel: Grandma's in the kitchen. She'll be very happy to see you.

Ernesto: What's for lunch?

Lourdes: Ernesto! My baby! My favorite grandson! Come here and give me a hug!

(*Ernesto is eating.*)

Isabel: Slow down, Ernesto! There's plenty of soup.

Ernesto: Sorry. I was starving. The food on the airplane was terrible.

Lourdes: Leave him alone, Isabel. My grandson is hungry, and he hasn't eaten home-cooked food in a long time.

Ernesto: You know, Grandma, we were all very worried about you. Nando and Margarita send their love. You really look good.

Isabel: So, Ernesto, what are you doing here?

Ernesto: Well, Margarita called me from New Jersey. She's worried about Mom. By the way, where is Mom?

Lourdes: Your mother is out with a friend. So, Margarita was worried about Ramona's date.

Ernesto: What do you mean date? I thought he was a friend. Tell me about him. She never goes out with anyone at home. Do you know the man?

Isabel: She's dating an old boyfriend named Vicente Fuentes.

Ernesto: What do you know about him? Is he nice? Does he have a good job?

Isabel: You sound like your grandfather, Ernesto. Your mother is a grown woman. She can take care of herself.

Vicente's Daughter

Get Ready to Read

A Discuss with a partner.

1. What is Ernesto doing?
2. How do you think Ramona feels right now?
3. What's going to happen next?

B Match the words and expressions with the definitions.

d	**1.** rude	**a.**	travel between two places: work and home
___	**2.** I don't mind.	**b.**	here's some more information
___	**3.** commute	**c.**	immediately after
___	**4.** in fact	**d.**	not polite
___	**5.** as soon as	**e.**	neat, in order
___	**6.** trust	**f.**	It doesn't bother me; it's not a problem.
___	**7.** well-organized	**g.**	believe in someone or something

In the last episode...

Ernesto arrived at his grandmother and aunt's house. Isabel told him about Ramona and Vicente's relationship, but no one knows why they broke up when they were in high school. Later, Ramona comes home and she brings Vicente with her. She is very surprised to see Ernesto. Everyone sits down for dinner, and after dinner Ernesto begins to question Vicente about his life.

Everyone is sitting on the patio waiting for coffee after dinner. Isabel is in the kitchen, and Ramona is sitting between Ernesto and Vicente. Ernesto begins to ask Vicente a lot of questions. "So, Vicente, why are you in Manzanillo? Don't you live in Texas? Do you have a family?"

"Ernesto!" says Ramona. "Don't be **rude**!"

At that moment, Isabel arrives with the coffee. She hands everyone a small cup of strong coffee.

"**Great timing**,* Isabel," says Ramona. "Ernesto is getting ready to interview Vicente."

"Where's my coffee?" asks Lourdes.

"Mami, coffee is not on your list. I made some herbal tea for you," says Isabel.

"How about some chocolate?" Lourdes asks.

"Sorry. Chocolate has caffeine, too."

"This new healthy plan is going to be hard," Lourdes complains. Everyone laughs.

"Back to you, Vicente. Why are you here in Manzanillo?" asks Ernesto.

"Ernesto, let Vicente drink his coffee," says Ramona.

"I **don't mind**, Ramona," says Vicente. "My daughter does the same thing."

"You have a daughter?" Ernesto, Isabel, and Lourdes all speak at the same time.

"Yes, I do. Would you like to see a picture?" Vicente asks.

"Yes, we would!" everyone answers. Everyone except Ramona moves closer to Vicente to see the picture. Ramona goes into the kitchen.

Vicente takes out his wallet and pulls out a picture. "This is Lupe. In this picture, she was only 18, but she's 36 now."

"She's beautiful, Vicente. Look at those green eyes," says Lourdes.

"Is she single?" asks Ernesto.

"Sorry, Ernesto. She's happily married and has a four-year-old son."

"She's 36? She's older than Nando, isn't she, Ramona?" says Lourdes. She looks around and doesn't see Ramona. "Ramona, where are you?"

"I'm in the kitchen," Ramona answers. She is reluctant to join them on the patio.

*__Great timing__ = *You did that at exactly the right time.* (In this case Ramona is serious, but the expression is often used to mean the opposite of what it says; for example, when someone arrives for a meeting so late that the meeting is finished, someone else might say, "Great timing.").

"Did you see this picture of Vicente's daughter?" asks Isabel. "She's very attractive."

"Yes, I saw it," answers Ramona.

Lourdes and Isabel look at each other. Then, they realize why Ramona is so quiet. Now they know why Ramona and Vicente broke up many years ago. Fortunately, Ernesto changes the subject.

"So, Vicente, you didn't answer my question. Why are you in town?"

"I'm here on business. I work for my father's company. I **commute** between San Antonio and Manzanillo a few days a month, sometimes more. **In fact**, I just bought a new house here. I was tired of staying in hotels, and now my daughter and her family live here, too. My son-in-law is also working in our Mexico office."

"Oh, really? You're in town a couple of days a month? I'm surprised we never ran into each other before," says Lourdes.

"So am I. Well, I have an early meeting tomorrow morning, and I have to leave. Thank you for the wonderful dinner. It was nice to see you again, Isabel and Mrs. Cruz, and it was great to meet you, Ernesto."

"I'll walk you to the door, Vicente," says Ramona. They go to the front door. **As soon as** they leave, Ernesto gets up and watches them from the patio.

"Sit down, Ernesto," says Lourdes. "Don't watch them."

"I don't **trust** him, Grandma," says Ernesto.

"Why not?" says Isabel. "He's very polite, and your mother likes him."

"I know. I just don't trust him," Ernesto says.

The next morning, Ramona, Lourdes, and Ernesto are walking to the center plaza. Every morning, Ramona walks with her mother to the plaza after Isabel goes to work. Lourdes needs to get more exercise, and Ramona's enjoying this time with her mother. Today, Ernesto is with them, too. Ramona is quiet this morning, so Ernesto is not going to talk about Vicente again. Ernesto knows that his mother is not comfortable talking about the relationship, especially about Vicente's daughter. He still has many questions, but he'll ask her later.

They are near the plaza when Ramona sees a florist's shop.

"Look, Mami. A new florist. That wasn't here before. I want to take a look. I'll meet you at the plaza."

"May I help you?" a young woman asks Ramona as she enters the florist.

"I was in the neighborhood, and I **noticed***this new shop. When did you open?"

"I opened about two months ago," says the woman.

"Well, it's a beautiful shop. I own a florist shop back in New Jersey."

"You do? Would you like to look around? It's not busy," the woman says. Ramona thinks the woman is very kind. The woman shows Ramona the workroom in the back of the store, where one woman is working on a bridal bouquet. Then the woman shows Ramona the different things that the shop sells. Everything is very **well-organized**, like Ramona's shop.

Ramona is very impressed. She says, "This is a very nice shop. It's in a great location, and your windows are beautiful. I'm sure your business will do well. Oh, that's a beautiful lily. I think I'll buy it for my mother."

While Ramona is paying for the plant, she notices a photo on the wall. "Is that your family?" she asks.

"Yes, it is," the woman answers. She takes down the photo and hands it to Ramona.

When Ramona looks at it, she is shocked. It's Vicente! "This must be Vicente's daughter, Lupe," she thinks to herself. "She has green eyes like her mother, Rosita. Who's the other woman in the picture?"

***notice** = see something or hear about something for the first time

The woman begins to describe the photo. "This is my father, Vicente, and my husband, Santos. He's an engineer. And this is my son, Luis. He'll be four on Saturday."

"Who's this?" Ramona asks, pointing at the woman in the photo.

"Oh, that's Claudia, my father's co-worker. She lives in Texas and used to be my grandfather's assistant. Now, she works with my father. She's very nice. She is like a mother to me. My mother left when I was just a baby, so my father and my grandparents raised me. My father works hard, but he's lonely. I hope that Claudia will become my stepmother. I know that she loves my father, but I don't know how he feels about her."

Ramona picks up her plant. "You . . . you have a beautiful family. Good luck with your shop, Lupe."

"Thank you," Lupe says. "How did you know my name? Wait, you didn't tell me your name." Lupe watches Ramona walking away. "That was strange," she thinks.

Ramona walks quickly down the street and turns the corner.

Reading Comprehension

A Circle *True* or *False.*

1. Ernesto has a lot of questions for Vicente. **True** **False**
2. Lourdes is going to have difficulty with her new food list. **True** **False**
3. Vicente's daughter is the same age as Nando. **True** **False**
4. Ramona wants to see Vicente's picture of his daughter. **True** **False**
5. Vicente works in both Mexico and Texas. **True** **False**
6. Vicente left the house because he was angry about Ernesto's questions. **True** **False**
7. Lourdes never saw Vicente when he was in town on business. **True** **False**
8. Ernesto feels uncomfortable about Vicente. **True** **False**

B Circle the correct answer.

1. Ramona, Ernesto, and Lourdes are going to the plaza because ________.
   - **a.** they want to have a serious discussion
   - **b.** they're going to eat breakfast
   - **c.** Lourdes needs exercise
   - **d.** there is a market at the plaza
2. Ramona wants to ________ the florist shop.
   - **a.** look around
   - **b.** buy
   - **c.** work at
   - **d.** get information about
3. When Ramona meets the woman in the florist shop, she ________.
   - **a.** wants to give her a job
   - **b.** doesn't like her
   - **c.** thinks that she knows her
   - **d.** likes her

4. Who is in the woman's photo?
   a. Vicente and his daughter
   b. Vicente, his son-in-law, and his grandson
   c. Vicente, Ramona, and his grandson
   d. Vicente, his son-in-law, his grandson, and a female friend

C Answer the questions.

1. Why did Ramona visit the florist? ____________________

   ____

2. Why was Ramona surprised when she looked at the photo?

   ____

3. Who is the woman in the photo? ____________________

4. Why did Ramona leave the florist? ____________________

   ____

Work with the Words

A Circle the correct answer.

1. The opposite of **rude** is ________.
   a. angry
   b. happy
   c. sad
   d. polite

2. **A:** Do you mind if I sit here?
   B: No, I **don't mind.** ________.
   a. Thank you
   b. Sit over there
   c. Don't sit down
   d. Please sit down

3. Mr. Lee **commutes** from his home to ________.
   a. his neighborhood
   b. his office
   c. the supermarket
   d. the bank

4. The Sears Tower is a very tall building. **In fact,** ________.
   a. it is a tall building
   b. it has many floors
   c. it is the tallest building in the United States
   d. it is 30 years old

5. **As soon as** Louise gets to work in the morning, she ________.
   a. checks her messages
   b. takes a break
   c. eats lunch
   d. goes home

6. I **trust** my neighbor to take care of my house when I'm away. He's very ________.
   a. false
   b. honest
   c. nosy
   d. talkative

7. The opposite of **well-organized** is ________.
   a. messy
   b. clean
   c. old
   d. new

8. "I didn't **notice** the stop sign" means ________.
   a. "I saw it"
   b. "I was paying attention to it"
   c. "The sign is new"
   d. "I didn't see it"

B Complete the sentences with the correct words and phrases.

as soon as	**I don't mind**	**notice**	**trust**
commute	**In fact**	**rude**	**well-organized**

1. **A:** Who are you going to hire?
   B: I don't know, but I need someone who is ______________. This office is so messy. I want to clean it up!

2. **A:** Can I borrow your dictionary? I forgot mine.
   B: Sure. ______________. I don't need it right now.

3. **A:** You look tired.
   B: I am. I just got home from work. I have to ______________ 40 miles each way every day.

4. **A:** When are you going to wash the car?
   B: I'll wash it ______________ I finish my homework.
5. **A:** Is that a new car?
   B: Yes, it is. ______________, it is my first new car. My other car was a used car.
6. **A:** There's a sale at the new department store. Do you want to go?
   B: No. I don't like the salespeople there. They are very ______________ to the customers.
7. **A:** Could you lend me five dollars? I'll pay it back tomorrow.
   B: Don't worry about it. I ______________ you. You can give it to me next week.
8. **A:** Excuse me, but you can't bring a dog in here! Didn't you see the sign?
   B: I'm sorry. I didn't ______________ the sign. It's very small.

Lifeskill Practice

Flowers for holidays and for every day

In the United States, people buy flowers for many occasions. For example, many people get flowers for their homes for Thanksgiving and Christmas. Valentine's Day is a popular day for men to give their girlfriends or wives flowers, especially red roses. Many people send flowers on birthdays and anniversaries, too. Some people send flowers when someone is sick.

Discuss the questions with a classmate.

- When do you give flowers?
- When was the last time that you received flowers?
- On what holidays are flowers popular?
- Which flowers do you like best?

Dialogue Practice

Practice the conversation with four classmates.

Ernesto: Back to you, Vicente. Why are you here in Manzanillo?

Ramona: Ernesto, let Vicente drink his coffee.

Vicente: I don't mind, Ramona. My daughter does the same thing.

Ernesto, Isabel, and Lourdes: You have a daughter?

Vicente: Yes, I do. Would you like to see a picture?

Ernesto, Isabel, and Lourdes: Yes, we would!

Vicente: This is Lupe. In this picture, she was only 18, but she's 36 now.

Lourdes: She's beautiful, Vicente. Look at those green eyes.

Ernesto: Is she single?

Vicente: Sorry, Ernesto. She's happily married and has a four-year old son.

Lourdes: She's 36? She's older than Nando, isn't she, Ramona? Ramona, where are you?

Ramona: I'm in the kitchen.

Isabel: Did you see this picture of Vicente's daughter? She's very attractive.

Ramona: Yes, I saw it.

A New Friend

Get Ready to Read

A **Discuss with a partner.**

1. Why does Ramona look upset?
2. Where is she going now?
3. Is Ramona going to tell her family about meeting Lupe?

B **Match the words and expressions with the definitions.**

_d_	1. realize	a. say hello
____	2. hurt	b. unusual; strange
____	3. greet	c. make someone feel bad
____	4. uneasy	d. understand; know
____	5. odd	e. stop working, usually at age 65
____	6. (be) supposed to	f. uncomfortable
____	7. retire	g. has to or expects to do something

In the last episode...

Ramona went to a new florist and talked to the owner of the shop. She found out that the owner was Lupe, Vicente's daughter. Ramona was surprised to meet her, but she didn't introduce herself. Ramona was looking at a photograph of Lupe's family when she learned that Vicente was dating another woman named Claudia. Lupe was hoping that Claudia would become her stepmother!

Ernesto and Lourdes are sitting on a bench in the central plaza. There is a fountain on one side, and in the center of the plaza there is a small bandshell where bands sometimes play in the evening and on weekends. People can sit, talk with friends, listen to music, or just relax in the plaza. Ernesto and Lourdes are talking and waiting for Ramona. Suddenly, they see a familiar face.

"Look, Ernesto!" says Lourdes. "There's Vicente. Let's say hello."

"Do we have to?" says Ernesto. He is reluctant to talk to Vicente, but he doesn't want to upset his grandmother.

"Come on," says Lourdes. She and Ernesto walk over to greet Vicente. He doesn't see them coming.

"Good morning, Vicente," says Lourdes.

Vicente is reading a newspaper. He looks up. He's surprised to see them, and he doesn't look happy. He is looking around the plaza. Then he stands up to **greet** them.

"Uh . . . Good morning, Mrs. Cruz, Ernesto. Thank you for the wonderful dinner last night."

"You're very welcome. Anytime. When you're in town, please call. You're like family, Vicente," says Lourdes.

Vicente looks **uneasy**. "Well, it was nice to see you." He shakes Ernesto's hand. "I have to go . . . "

"Grandpa! Look!" A little boy comes running up to Vicente. He's holding a toy snake. "Look at this! Auntie Claudia bought it for me."

Vicente picks up the boy and says to Ernesto and Lourdes. "This is my grandson, Luis. Luis, these are my friends, Mrs. Cruz and her grandson, Ernesto."

An attractive older woman joins Vicente. "Vicente, introduce me to your friends."

Vicente looks very uncomfortable. He introduces the woman. "Claudia, these are old family friends from Texas. Mrs. Cruz, this is my . . . friend, Claudia

Walker. She was my father's assistant until he **retired**. Claudia, this is Lourdes Cruz and her grandson, Ernesto."

Claudia is in her late fifties. She's attractive and blond. She's wearing a brightly colored dress and heels. "So how do you know Vicente, Mrs. Cruz?"

"Oh, we're old friends from San Antonio. I'm living here in Manzanillo now with my oldest daughter. My youngest daughter, Ramona, and Vicente . . . "

Vicente interrupts. "Look at the time! I'm sorry, I didn't **realize** it was so late. We have to go. We're meeting my daughter for lunch. See you soon."

"It was nice meeting you both. Come on, Luis." Claudia takes Luis's hand and starts to leave.

"Bye, bye!" says Luis.

"Bye!" says Lourdes. Lourdes and Ernesto watch them leave.

"That was **odd**. Vicente was in a hurry to leave, wasn't he?"

"He sure was. In fact, he couldn't leave fast enough. What do you think about Claudia?" asks Ernesto.

"Well, I don't think she's just a friend. She seemed very comfortable with Vicente and his grandson. He called her Aunt Claudia."

"You're right. Do you think she knows about Mom?"

"I don't know, Ernesto. What should we tell your mother?"

"If we tell Mom, she might get upset. She's **supposed to** go out with Vicente tonight, isn't she? Maybe she already knows about Claudia. Let's wait. Maybe she'll tell us what's going on. Vicente had better not **hurt** Mom. I think she really likes him, Grandma."

"I think you're right. Look, here comes your mother." Lourdes calls to Ramona, and Ramona comes in their direction. She looks like she is thinking about something else.

"Mom, are you OK?" asks Ernesto. "You look strange."

"I'm fine, sweetie," answers Ramona. "Here, Mami. I bought you a plant for the patio."

"Oh, it's beautiful. How was the florist? Was it as nice as yours?"

Ramona says, "It was OK. Guess what? Lupe, Vicente's daughter, is the owner and runs that floral shop."

"You're kidding," says Ernesto. "Is she as beautiful as her picture?"

"First of all, she's married, and yes, she's very beautiful," answers Ramona.

"Did you introduce yourself, Ramona? She probably knows all about you."

Ramona lies. "No, she was very busy. We didn't have time to talk."

"Mom, you're too quiet. What's up?"

"Well, I think that maybe it is time for me to go back home."

"What?" says Lourdes. "Why now?"

"I came here more than three weeks ago. You're doing fine, and you have Isabel to take care of you. I have to get back to my business, and I miss Mambo."

Lourdes frowns. "Ramona, you can bring Mambo here, and you can open a florist anywhere. Maybe right here in Manzanillo. What about that? And what about Vicente? He'll be disappointed."

Ramona looks at her mother and son. "Vicente is just an old friend. We've been having fun talking about old times. But open a florist here? Move here? What about my life back in New Jersey?"

Lourdes says, "You can have a life here, too, Ramona. Think about it."

Ramona gets up. "Let's talk about that later. Let's go home. I'm getting hungry."

As they are walking back, Ernesto and Lourdes see that Ramona is unusually quiet. They look at each other. They are thinking the same thing, "Does she know about Claudia?"

Reading Comprehension

A Circle *True* or *False.*

1. Vicente notices Ernesto and Lourdes first. **True** **False**
2. Vicente is happy to introduce his friend Claudia. **True** **False**
3. Claudia is pleased to meet Lourdes and Ernesto. **True** **False**
4. Vicente leaves quickly. **True** **False**
5. Ernesto and Lourdes think Vicente was uncomfortable. **True** **False**
6. Ernesto and Lourdes are going to tell Ramona about Claudia. **True** **False**
7. Lourdes thinks Ramona should return to New Jersey. **True** **False**
8. Ramona tells Lourdes and Ernesto about Claudia. **True** **False**

B Circle the correct answer.

1. Ramona is ________ when she joins her son and mother.

   a. crying **c.** upset
   b. happy **d.** quiet

2. Ramona told Ernesto that Lupe was ________.

   a. nice **c.** unfriendly
   b. like her picture **d.** not at her florist shop

3. Lourdes is ________ that Ramona wants to return home.

   a. not surprised **c.** confused
   b. excited **d.** upset

4. Who talked about Claudia with Ramona?

   a. Vicente **c.** Lourdes
   b. Ernesto **d.** Lupe

C Who does the sentence describe? You may use some names more than once.

Claudia	Lourdes	Luis	Ramona	Vicente

1. ______________ was feeling uncomfortable.
2. ______________ was excited about a present.
3. ______________ used to work for Vicente's father.
4. ______________ is thinking about leaving town.
5. ______________ and ______________ are concerned about Ramona.
6. ______________ and ______________ are confused about Claudia.

Work with the Words

A Circle the correct answer.

1. I missed my bus because I didn't **realize** that ________.
   - **a.** the bus was full
   - **b.** I had to take a bus
   - **c.** it was raining
   - **d.** I was at the wrong bus stop
2. "I hope I didn't **hurt** you" means ________.
   - **a.** you injured me
   - **b.** I didn't want to make you feel bad
   - **c.** someone made me
   - **d.** someone made you feel bad
3. She was **uneasy** at her job interview because she was ________.
   - **a.** well-prepared
   - **b.** confident
   - **c.** not prepared
   - **d.** on time
4. My dog is so friendly! He always ________ everyone who comes to the house.
   - **a.** sees
   - **b.** bites
   - **c.** feeds
   - **d.** greets

5. The opposite of **odd** is ________.
   - **a.** normal
   - **b.** easy
   - **c.** unusual
   - **d.** simple

6. A good student **is supposed to** ________.
   - **a.** come to class prepared
   - **b.** miss classes
   - **c.** do all assignments
   - **d.** both a and c

7. She **retired** because she ________.
   - **a.** got a better job
   - **b.** had an argument with her boss
   - **c.** didn't like her job
   - **d.** worked for 30 years

B Complete the sentences with the correct words and phrases. You will not use all the words.

hurt	**odd**	**reluctant**	**uneasy**
greet	**realize**	**retire**	**were supposed to**

1. She was very ______________ when she arrived at the party because she didn't know anyone there.
2. My neighbors ______________ go on vacation last week, but their son became sick, so they couldn't go.
3. I am ______________ to buy a new car. My company is not doing well right now.
4. **A:** Excuse me, but I think you have my notebook.

   B: Oh, I'm sorry. I didn't ______________ that yours was the same color.
5. **A:** Why isn't your sister talking to you?

   B: We had a fight, and I ______________ her feelings.
6. The weather is very ______________ today. It doesn't usually rain at this time of year.

Lifeskill Practice

Thanking someone

Vicente says, "Thank you for the wonderful dinner last night." Lourdes answers, "You're very welcome. Anytime." There are many possible answers to "Thank you":

You're welcome.	No problem.	It's my pleasure.
Don't mention it.	My pleasure.	Anytime.

A Practice the conversations with a classmate.

1. **A:** Thank you for your help.
   B: No problem.
2. **A:** Thanks for inviting me to lunch.
   B: My pleasure.
3. **A:** Thank you for picking me up.
   B: Don't mention it.

B Write a new conversation and practice it with a classmate.

Dialogue Practice

Practice the conversation with three classmates.

Lourdes: Good morning, Vicente.

Vicente: Uh . . . Good morning, Mrs. Cruz, Ernesto. Thank you for the wonderful dinner last night.

Lourdes: You're very welcome. Anytime. When you're in town, please call. You're like family, Vicente.

Vicente: Well, it was nice to see you. I have to go . . .

Luis: Grandpa! Look! Look at this! Auntie Claudia bought it for me.

Vicente: This is my grandson, Luis. Luis, these are my friends, Mrs. Cruz and her grandson, Ernesto.

Claudia: Vicente, introduce me to your friends.

Vicente: Claudia, these are old family friends from Texas. Mrs. Cruz, this is my . . . friend, Claudia Walker. She was my father's assistant until he retired. Claudia, this is Lourdes Cruz and her grandson, Ernesto.

Claudia: So how do you know Vicente, Mrs. Cruz?

Lourdes: Oh, we're old friends from San Antonio. I'm living here in Manzanillo now with my oldest daughter. My youngest daughter, Ramona, and Vicente . . .

Vicente: Look at the time! I'm sorry, I didn't realize it was so late. We have to go. We're meeting my daughter for lunch. See you soon.

Claudia: It was nice meeting you both. Come on, Luis.

Luis: Bye, bye!

Lourdes: Bye!

A Decision

Get Ready to Read

A **Discuss with a partner.**

1. What is Ramona thinking about?
2. What are Lourdes and Ernesto thinking about?
3. Are Lourdes and Ernesto going to say anything about Claudia?

B **Match the words and expressions with the definitions.**

__g__ **1.** convince someone
____ **2.** be used to
____ **3.** admit
____ **4.** take out
____ **5.** complain
____ **6.** cheer up
____ **7.** pretend

a. agree that something is true or correct
b. make someone happier
c. pay for someone's meal in a restaurant or other entertainments
d. have the habit of doing something
e. act as if something is true
f. say that you do not like something
g. make someone do something or agree with you

In the last episode...

Ernesto and Lourdes were waiting for Ramona in the plaza when they ran into Vicente. They tried to greet him, but he was very uneasy and he left very quickly. He was with his grandson and a woman named Claudia. She seemed very close to Vicente and his grandson. Ernesto and Lourdes decided not to say anything about Claudia to Ramona. When Ramona returned, she didn't tell them that she knew about Claudia, too. Ramona surprised her mother when she said that she was thinking about returning to New Jersey.

That evening, Ramona and her family are at home. Ramona is thinking about going back to New Jersey. Isabel and Lourdes are trying to **convince** her to stay a little longer. They **are used to** having her there. They think that she wants to leave because of Vicente, but Ramona says that she needs to get back to her business. Then, Vicente calls.

Ramona answers the phone, "Hello?"

Vicente says, "Hi, Ramona. How are you? How was your day?"

Ramona answers, "It was interesting. My mother, Ernesto, and I went to the plaza. By the way, I met your daughter."

Vicente is surprised. "You met Lupe? Where? She didn't say anything."

Ramona says, "I met her at her florist shop. I didn't introduce myself." Ramona lies, "We didn't have time to talk. She was busy."

"Oh, really?" Vicente sounds relieved to hear that Lupe doesn't know who Ramona is. He changes the subject. "Ramona, I'm calling to say that I won't be able to see you tonight. I have an unexpected meeting."

"A meeting? So late? Well, that's OK. I have a lot to think about."

Vicente's interested. "What are you thinking about?"

"I'm thinking about going back home. I need to get back to my business."

Vicente sounds a little anxious. "When are you going to leave?"

Ramona waits, and then she answers, "As soon as I can make a reservation. I think I'll make some calls tonight."

Vicente says, "Tonight? What's the hurry?"

Ramona thinks for a few seconds. Then she says, "Vicente, my mother's improving every day. Isabel is going to take a **leave of absence*** to take care of her. I feel confident that I can leave now."

Then Vicente says, "But, Ramona, we were getting to know each other again. Can't we talk about this?"

Ramona gets a little angry, "What do we have to talk about? Lupe told me about your friend Claudia. In fact, Lupe's hoping that Claudia will become her stepmother."

Vicente is surprised to hear that Ramona knows about Claudia. "Stepmother? I never . . . "

"I'm sorry, Vicente. I have to go, and you have a meeting, don't you? It was nice to see you again. Good-bye." Ramona hangs up the phone.

***leave of absence** = time off from a job, not paid

After Ramona hangs up, Vicente calls back a few more times, but Ramona doesn't answer the phone. Then she tells her family about Claudia. Lourdes and Ernesto **admit** that they met Claudia at the plaza that morning.

Ernesto is angry. "See, Grandma, I told you that I didn't trust him."

Ramona is curious about Claudia, so Ernesto describes her. "Well, she is probably about the same age as Vicente and you, Mom."

Isabel asks, "Come on! What did she look like?"

Lourdes says, "She was blonde, thin, and was wearing too much makeup. But, she seemed nice."

Ramona doesn't say anything at first. "I think this is a good time for me to go home. I'm going to make some calls and try to leave tomorrow."

Lourdes says, "Tomorrow? Ramona, you're not leaving tomorrow, especially because of Vicente. Anyway, you **owe**[*] me a birthday lunch."

Ramona looks at her mother. "What are you talking about? Your birthday was two months ago."

Lourdes answers, "Ramona, you didn't visit me on my birthday. So, you owe me a birthday lunch."

"OK, I can't argue with you. I'll **take you out** tomorrow afternoon, but I'm going to leave the day after tomorrow. Isabel, call the neighbors and Mom's close friends. I'll take everybody to La Casa de los Mariscos. That's your favorite restaurant, isn't it, Mami?"

"Yes, it is. And, make sure my favorite waiter is working at our table."

"OK, OK," Ramona says. "But, remember, you can't eat too much. You have to follow the nutritionist's advice." Ramona is in a much better mood now.

"Oh, you're no fun," **complains** Lourdes.

* * * *

The next day Lourdes, Isabel, Ernesto, and Ramona are sitting at a table near the window at Lourdes's favorite restaurant, La Casa de los Mariscos. "Welcome, Mrs. Cruz. It's nice to see you again," says the owner. It is clear that Lourdes knows everybody. The waiters bring some chips and salsa to the table. Ernesto is tasting everything, but Isabel immediately moves the chips away from her mother. Lourdes looks very disappointed. The owner is standing at the table making sure that everything's OK. "Would you like anything to drink?"

[*]**owe** = need to return or repay a favor or money

"No, thank you, Chano. We'll wait for the rest of our party to arrive. But you could bring us some water," says Lourdes.

"Right away, Mrs. Cruz." The owner tells a waiter to bring water to the table.

Lourdes looks at Ramona. "Ramona, I'm going to miss you when you go home."

Ramona looks a little sad, "It's hard to leave, Mami. I'm going to miss you and Isabel, too. Don't worry. You know I'll call often."

Isabel says, "Ramona, did you think about what we said? How about opening a shop here in Manzanillo? There are many opportunities here."

"But, Isabel," says Ramona. "I think I would feel a little uncomfortable. You know, because of Vicente."

Ernesto looks at his mother. "Don't worry about him, Mom. Remember he said that he travels a lot. He has a house here, but he lives in San Antonio most of the time. His daughter is here, but she doesn't know who you are. You were here for two weeks before you ran into Vicente. Listen, you're still young. I'll tell you what you always tell me when I break up with a woman, '**There are plenty of fish in the sea.**' "*

Ramona laughs and kisses Ernesto on the cheek. "You always know how to **cheer me up**, Ernesto." Then Ramona says, "Oh, no. Look who's here."

Isabel looks first. "Who is it? Do you know her?"

Lourdes looks and then explains, "Isabel, that's Claudia. That's the woman that we were talking about. I wonder who she's waiting for."

*__There are plenty of fish in the sea.__ = (idiom) *There are lots of other nice people to meet and date.*

Isabel whispers to her mother, "You were right about the makeup."

Claudia is sitting at a table on the other side of the restaurant. She is sitting at a table for four, but the other chairs are empty.

"Excuse me," Ramona says. She gets up and goes to the restroom.

Lourdes watches Ramona leave. "Isabel, is she OK?"

Isabel says, "Let's give her a couple of minutes. If she doesn't come back, I'll go get her."

In the restroom, Ramona washes her hands. Then she looks in her purse for her lipstick. The door opens, and someone comes in. It's Claudia Walker! "So you're Ramona," says Claudia. She is staring at Ramona. She looks angry.

Ramona **pretends** that she doesn't know who Claudia is. "Excuse me, do we know each other?"

"Let me introduce myself, but I think you know who I am. I'm Claudia Walker, Vicente's girlfriend."

"Really?" says Ramona. "Vicente never mentioned you or a girlfriend."

"Well, Vicente never mentioned his high school girlfriend until last night."

Ramona speaks nervously, "Last night? I thought Vicente had a business meeting."

"Vicente and I work together," says Claudia. "So, Ramona, are you trying to start over with Vicente after all these years?"

"That's between Vicente and me, Ms. Walker," says Ramona.

"No, it isn't. I'm planning a life with Vicente and his family. I'm like a mother to Lupe, and I spend all my holidays with Vicente and his family. I'm part of the family."

"You are? So why has Vicente been spending all of his evenings with me? He was at my mother's house just the other night. Our families have known each other a long time." Ramona is getting angry.

"Oh, really? That was a long time ago. Things are different now. I'm part of Vicente's family, and I expect to be the next Mrs. Fuentes."

"I don't have time for this. My family is waiting for me. I think you're dreaming, Ms. Walker. If Vicente is serious about you, why doesn't he want me to leave? I think you and your *boyfriend* should have a serious talk." Ramona walks out of the restroom and bumps into Isabel.

"Ramona, I saw that woman follow you in here. Is everything OK?" Isabel asks.

"Everything's fine. Let's eat." Ramona says.

About five minutes later, Ramona and her family and friends are sitting at the table. Ramona stands up to **make a toast**.* "Thank you all for coming. This is supposed to be my birthday lunch to my mother, but I think it should be a recovery lunch. All of us were very worried about my mother, but as you can see, she's doing very well. To my mother's continued good health! Cheers!"

Everyone lifts their glasses and toasts Lourdes. The waiters clap, too.

***make a toast** = raise a glass and say "Cheers!" or make a speech wishing someone good luck; often at a wedding or other celebration

At that moment, Vicente, Lupe, and Luis come into the restaurant. The first thing Vicente sees is Ramona standing at her table with her family. The second thing he sees is Claudia sitting alone at her table. Claudia jumps up from her table and runs over to greet Vicente. "Vicente, honey!" She kisses him and hugs him in front of everybody!

Reading Comprehension

A Circle *True* or *False.*

1. Isabel and Lourdes want Ramona to go back home. **True** **False**
2. Lupe told Vicente about Ramona. **True** **False**
3. Vicente is busy with his family tonight. **True** **False**
4. Ramona is angry at Vicente. **True** **False**
5. Ramona is going to leave in one week. **True** **False**
6. Many of the workers at the restaurant know Lourdes. **True** **False**
7. Ramona is seriously thinking about opening a new shop. **True** **False**
8. Ernesto thinks his mother should date other men. **True** **False**

B Circle the correct answer.

1. Ramona was surprised to see ________ in the restroom.
   - **a.** Isabel
   - **b.** Lourdes
   - **c.** Claudia
   - **d.** Lupe
2. Claudia believes that ________ will marry Vicente.
   - **a.** Ramona
   - **b.** Isabel
   - **c.** no one
   - **d.** she
3. Ramona doesn't believe that Vicente ________.
   - **a.** is in love with Claudia
   - **b.** lives in both Mexico and Texas
   - **c.** works with Claudia
   - **d.** knows Claudia
4. Vicente comes to the restaurant to have lunch with ________.
   - **a.** Lourdes and her family
   - **b.** Ramona
   - **c.** his family and Claudia
   - **d.** a business associate

C Who said it? Write the name of the person.

Claudia **Ernesto** **Isabel** **Lourdes** **Ramona** **Vicente**

1. ______________ "I need to get back to my business."
2. ______________ "You owe me a birthday lunch."
3. ______________ "She was blonde, thin, and was wearing too much makeup."
4. ______________ "There are plenty of fish in the sea."
5. ______________ "If she doesn't come back, I'll go get her."
6. ______________ "Things are different now."
7. ______________ "I'm planning a life with Vicente and his family."
8. ______________ "What's the hurry?"

Work with the Words

A Circle the correct answer.

1. The price of the car is very low. The salesman **convinced** me to ________ it.

   a. sell **c.** fix
   b. buy **d.** keep

2. When I first moved to Chicago, I **wasn't used to** the cold ________, and I had to buy new clothes.

   a. airport **c.** weather
   b. food **d.** language

3. I gave Jack $25 to buy a textbook last week. He gave me $15 yesterday, so now he **owes** me ________.

   a. a book **c.** $25
   b. $10 **d.** nothing

4. Kim **complained** about the new restaurant. She said the food was ________.

   a. delicious
   b. new
   c. hot
   d. bad

5. After Mr. Smith's operation, ________ **cheered him up**.

   a. the hospital food
   b. another operation
   c. a visit from his grandchildren
   d. a noisy roommate

6. The car thief **admitted** that the car wasn't ________.

   a. working
   b. new
   c. old
   d. his

7. Mr. Smith's grandson loves dogs, and sometimes he **pretends** that he is ________.

   a. a cat
   b. Mr. Smith
   c. a puppy
   d. a boy

8. It's your birthday! I'm going to ________.

   a. take you out
   b. take you to work
   c. run into you
   d. break up with you

B **Complete the conversations with the correct words and phrases.**

admit	**convince**	**owe**
aren't used to	**is complaining**	**pretend**
cheer her up	**make a toast**	**take her out**

1. **A:** What can we do to ______________?

   B: How about taking her to the movies?

2. **A:** What's wrong?

   B: The customer ______________ about the high prices.

3. **A:** How much do I ______________ for the repairs?

   B: $125, please.

4. **A:** Didn't you hear me? I was shouting your name.

   B: I was trying to ______________ that I didn't hear you. I don't want to talk to anyone right now.

5. **A:** Why are they wearing their coats today? I don't think it's so cold!

   B: They're from Florida. They ______________ to the weather here.

6. **A:** Why is everyone standing up?

   B: It's time to ______________ to the bride and groom.

7. **A:** Why did you do so poorly on the exam?

   B: I don't know, but I ______________ that I didn't study very hard.

8. **A:** Come on! It's going to be a great movie. How can I ______________ you to come with us?

   B: You can pay for my ticket.

9. **A:** It's Lucy's last day at work before she retires. What should we do?

   B: Let's ______________ to lunch.

Lifeskill Practice

Time off work

There are different reasons we take time off from work.

Isabel is going to take a **leave of absence** to take care of her mother.

A **Match the expressions with their definitions.**

____ 1. leave of absence

____ 2. vacation

____ 3. sick leave

____ 4. personal day

____ 5. maternity leave

a. time off (short, paid) for personal reasons

b. time off (paid) to take care of a new baby

c. time off (paid) when you are sick

d. time off (long, unpaid)

e. time off once a year (paid), sometimes to take a trip

B **Talk with a classmate about a job you had in the past. How much time off did you get?**

Dialogue Practice

Practice the conversation with a classmate.

Vicente: What are you thinking about?

Ramona: I'm thinking about going back home. I need to get back to my business.

Vicente: When are you going to leave?

Ramona: As soon as I can make a reservation. I think I'll make some calls tonight.

Vicente: Tonight? What's the hurry?

Ramona: Vicente, my mother's improving every day. Isabel is going to take a leave of absence to take care of her. I feel confident that I can leave now.

Vicente: But, Ramona, we were getting to know each other again. Can't we talk about this?

Ramona: What do we have to talk about? Lupe told me about your friend Claudia. In fact, Lupe's hoping that Claudia will become her stepmother.

Vicente: Stepmother? I never . . .

Ramona: I'm sorry, Vicente. I have to go, and you have a meeting, don't you? It was nice to see you again. Good-bye.

Time to Go Home

Get Ready to Read

A Discuss with a partner.

1. What is happening at the restaurant?
2. How do you think Ramona feels?
3. What is going to happen next?

B Match the words and expressions with the definitions.

_f_	1. put off	a. make a final decision
____	2. give someone a piece of your mind	b. say that you are sorry
		c. know someone's face
____	3. apologize	d. tell someone that you are very angry with him or her
____	4. drop by	
____	5. recognize	e. kind; does things for others
____	6. make up one's mind	f. change something to a later date
____	7. considerate	g. visit without calling first or without an invitation

In the last episode...

Ramona decided to **put off** her return trip for two days. She took Lourdes, Isabel, and Ernesto to Lourdes's favorite restaurant, La Casa de los Mariscos. They were waiting for the other guests when Ramona noticed Claudia, Vicente's friend, sitting at another table. Ramona went into the restroom, and Claudia followed her. Claudia told Ramona that she expected to become Vicente's wife. Ramona told Claudia that Vicente didn't want her to go back home to New Jersey and left. A few minutes later, after Ramona finished making a toast to her mother, Vicente, his daughter, and his grandson came into the restaurant. Claudia jumped up and ran to Vicente.

Ramona is looking at Vicente and Claudia. Everyone at Ramona's table is looking at Vicente and Claudia. No one is talking. Isabel finally says, "Ramona, sit down. Don't pay any attention to them."

Lourdes tries to break the silence and speaks up, "Vicente! We didn't expect to run into you today. Would you and your family like to join us for lunch? We're celebrating my birthday, a few months late." Lourdes laughs, and the rest of her guests laugh, too. Ramona sits down.

Claudia is holding Vicente's arm. Lupe looks surprised to see Ramona again. Luis points at Lourdes and speaks first, "Hi! You're the lady in the plaza. Don't you remember, Grandpa?"

Vicente looks very nervous and embarrassed. "I'm sorry, Mrs. Cruz. Let me introduce my daughter. Lupe, these are some old friends from San Antonio, Mrs. Lourdes Cruz, and her daughters, Isabel Molina, and Ramona Rivera. This is Ramona's son, Ernesto."

Lupe looks at Ramona and says, "Oh, I remember you. You came into my shop yesterday, didn't you? I think you bought a lily."

Ramona says, "Oh, yes. You look familiar. That's a very nice shop. My mother is enjoying her lily." Ramona looks nervous and uncomfortable.

Claudia interrupts, "I'm Claudia Walker, a friend of the family." She shakes hands with Ramona, and Vicente looks nervous. Claudia looks at Ernesto and Lourdes and says, "We met yesterday in the plaza. How nice to see you again." Ernesto and Lourdes try to be polite. They smile at her.

Vicente speaks to Lourdes, "I'm sorry, Mrs. Cruz. We are a little late. We're going to have a quick lunch and leave. Claudia and I have to go to a meeting this afternoon. Please, have a nice lunch." Vicente kisses Lourdes on the cheek and leads his family and Claudia to their table.

Isabel whispers to Ramona, "Are you OK? You didn't say anything."

"Isabel, I'm fine. Let's finish our lunch," says Ramona, and she calls the owner, who comes to the table right away. He realizes that something strange is happening. "Chano, the waiters can start bringing the food. Everyone's here."

"Fine, Mrs. Rivera," says Chano. He walks away to give instructions to the waiters.

"I hope you're all hungry," says Ramona. "The food here is delicious!" Ramona is beginning to relax, so everyone else begins talking again.

* * * *

Later that evening Ramona is packing. Everyone's in her room talking about what happened at lunch. Ernesto is angry. "I can't believe that Claudia pretended not to know you, Mom. **Who is she kidding**?"*

Lourdes says, "Relax, Ernesto. Sometimes this happens. I'm sure that Vicente didn't know that we were going to be there, too. His daughter seemed very nice, and I like his grandson, Luis."

Isabel is angry, too. "Ramona, aren't you angry? You should give Vicente **a piece of your mind**. He should know how you feel."

Ernesto asks, "What are you going to do now, Mom?"

Ramona thinks for a minute. Then she gets up and walks to the patio. She looks outside. It's a beautiful evening. She says, "You know, I'm very glad that Mami is doing well. It's time for me to go home. I'm not going to think about Vicente and his family. If he decides to marry Claudia, that's his business. I'm not going to worry about it."

Suddenly, there's a knock at the door. Lourdes looks at Ramona. "I wonder who that is. People don't usually **drop by** without calling."

Isabel answers the door. "What do *you* want?"

Vicente speaks nervously, "I'd like to speak to Ramona. Is she still here?"

Isabel calls Ramona, "Ramona, it's for you."

Ramona comes to the door, and Ernesto is standing behind her. "Is everything OK, Mom?" He's staring at Vicente.

Ramona looks at Ernesto. "Everything's fine, honey. I'm just going to take a short walk with Vicente. I'll be right back. Come on, Vicente. Let's take a walk."

*__Who is she kidding?__ (idiom) = *Is she serious?*

Vicente immediately begins to **apologize**. "I'm sorry about lunch today, and I'm sorry that I didn't tell you about Claudia. I never wanted to hurt you."

"I understand, Vicente," says Ramona. "But it doesn't matter now. I'm going home tomorrow."

"Tomorrow?" says Vicente. "But what about us?"

"Vicente, there is no 'us,'" she says. "What about Claudia?"

"Claudia is just a friend. I don't love her. I still love you, Ramona," says Vicente. "As soon as I saw you at the market, all of those old feelings returned. We can start over."

Ramona looks at Vicente. Then she takes his hands and speaks, "I don't think so, Vicente. We were just teenagers before. Now, we are parents and grandparents. My life is in New Jersey. I have a business, and two of my children are there. I have grandchildren, there, too. **I've made up my mind**. I'm going home."

"But, Ramona," says Vicente, "I still love you."

"No, you don't, Vicente," says Ramona. "You love your 17-year-old high school sweetheart. We're not 17 anymore. We both have responsibilities, and I'm not going to change my life for you. Be honest. You were thinking about marrying Claudia before we ran into each other at the market."

"That's true. I was lonely. I don't love Claudia, but I like her. She's good to Luis and Lupe. They really love her."

"Be happy with Claudia, Vicente," says Ramona.

"Can I call you when you come for a visit?" asks Vicente.

"I don't think that's a good idea. Maybe we will run into each other in town, and then we can talk as friends."

"As friends," says Vicente. "So that's it. I should go. Good night, Ramona."

"Good-bye, Vicente," says Ramona, and she goes back into the house.

* * * *

When Ramona arrives in New Jersey the next day, Margarita is not at the airport to pick her up. "Maybe Margarita's at work. I'll take a taxi." Ramona is standing in the taxi line. Suddenly, she hears her name, "Mrs. Rivera! Over here!" It's Mr. Martinez, her second-floor tenant. He's standing in front of his car, and her dog, Mambo, is in the back seat barking and jumping around the car.

"I'm sorry I'm late. Your daughter is busy at work, so she asked me to pick you up. How's your mother?"

Mr. Martinez takes Ramona's suitcases and puts them in the trunk of the car. Mambo is happy to see Ramona. She's jumping all over the car.

"My mother is fine, Mr. Martinez. Thank you for asking. I'm so happy that you brought Mambo. I missed her. I hope she wasn't too much trouble."

"She wasn't any trouble, Mrs. Rivera," says Mr. Martinez. "Mambo and I are great friends now. Everyone missed you, too." He's smiling. He opens the door for her, and Ramona gets into the car.

On the way home, Ramona asks Mr. Martinez lots of questions about the house and the neighbors. They talk comfortably.

When they get back to the house, Ramona notices a lot of cars on the street, but it's dark, so she doesn't **recognize** any of the cars. "The street is crowded. Why don't you get out here, in front of the house? I can look for a parking space and bring your suitcase," says Mr. Martinez.

"Thanks a lot. You're right. It *is* very crowded tonight," says Ramona. She gets out of the car with Mambo and walks up the steps to her front porch. "Hmm. The front porch light is out. I'll have to fix that tomorrow."

Ramona is getting out her keys when Mambo starts barking and **growling**.* "What's the matter, Mambo?"

Suddenly, the door opens. "It's hard to surprise you! Welcome home, Mom!" It's Ramona's daughter, Margarita. "How's Grandma?" Margarita hugs and kisses Ramona. Mambo stops barking and is wagging his tail.

Ramona's son, Fernando, and his wife and children are there, too. "It's good to have you back, Mom. I thought we were going to have to go to Mexico and bring you back ourselves! We missed you!"

"I missed you, too," says Ramona.

***growl** = noise a dog makes when it is angry or frightened

Nelly hugs Ramona and says,"Ramona, it's about time! All of the customers are asking about you. They were wondering if you were going to sell the shop. I told them that they must all be crazy."

"You're right, Nelly," says Ramona, laughing. "I am not selling the shop. Whose idea was this party? Oh, and there's so much food! Great! I'm hungry!" says Ramona.

"Well, Mr. Martinez, Nando, and I planned it," says Margarita. "Mr. Martinez ordered the food, I did the decorations, and Nando called everybody. Nelly brought the flowers. You know, Mom, Mr. Martinez was very helpful to me while you were away. He was very **considerate**. He knew I was worried about you, so he took care of everything here at the house. I didn't have to worry about anything but you and Grandma. You didn't answer my question. How's Grandma?"

"She's doing very well, sweetie," says Ramona. "She and Aunt Isabel send their love."

Then Mr. Martinez comes in with the suitcases. "So how do you like your surprise, Mrs. Rivera?"

"It's a wonderful surprise and, please, call me Ramona." Ramona smiles.

"And, please, call me Gabriel." Mr. Martinez has a big smile on his face, too.

"Mom," says Margarita, "what about that old boyfriend? Ernesto called me and told me everything about a man named Vicente."

"Vicente who?" says Ramona. "Come on, Gabriel, let's get something to eat."

Reading Comprehension

A Circle *True* or *False*.

1. Lupe has a fight with Vicente.	True	False
2. Vicente introduces his daughter to Ramona.	True	False
3. Lupe is surprised to see Ramona again.	True	False
4. Ramona relaxes after seeing Vicente.	True	False
5. Ernesto is angry about Vicente and Claudia.	True	False
6. Lourdes wants Ramona to marry Vicente.	True	False
7. Isabel and Ernesto feel the same about Vicente.	True	False
8. Ramona hopes to marry Vicente.	True	False

B Circle the correct answer.

1. When Vicente arrives at Lourdes's house, he feels ________.
   a. anxious
   b. confident
   c. relaxed
   d. confused
2. According to Vicente, Claudia is ________.
   a. his next wife
   b. a neighbor
   c. his daughter's mother
   d. a friend of the family
3. Ramona doesn't want to have a relationship with Vicente because ________.
   a. she is in love with him
   b. she has a life in New Jersey
   c. she is in love with another man
   d. she likes Claudia
4. The next time that Ramona comes to visit her mother and sister, she ________.
   a. will call Vicente
   b. won't talk to Vicente
   c. will open a new floral shop
   d. will be polite to Vicente if she sees him

C **Answer the questions.**

1. Why did Ramona come to Manzanillo?

   She came to Manzanillo because ______________________________

   ____

2. Why did Ernesto come to Manzanillo?

   He came to Manzanillo because ______________________________

   ____

3. Who took care of Ramona's business while she was away?

   ____

4. How does Claudia Walker know Vicente? ______________

   ____

5. Why didn't Vicente marry Claudia before? ______________

   ____

6. Why did Mr. Martinez bring Mambo with him to the airport?

   ____

7. What do you think is going to happen next? ______________

   ____

Work with the Words

A **Circle the correct answer.**

1. My mother often **drops by** my house in the afternoons because ________.

   a. college was too hard for her
   b. she doesn't have a car
   c. we get along really well
   d. she doesn't like to talk

2. Ramona was **relieved** after ________.

   a. she met Claudia
   b. her mother left the hospital
   c. she left New Jersey
   d. her mother became sick

3. Vicente wanted to **apologize** because he felt bad about ________.

a. Claudia
b. his daughter
c. his grandson
d. Lourdes

4. Lupe **recognized** ________ at the restaurant.

a. her father
b. Ramona
c. Ernesto
d. everyone

5. Mr. Martinez was very **considerate** to Margarita. He ________.

a. helped her when she needed it
b. never answered her phone calls
c. has a lot of friends
d. couldn't pick up Ramona

6. Ramona's **mind was made up**. She decided to ________.

a. marry Vicente
b. open a store in Manzanillo
c. go back home
d. make friends with Claudia

7. Isabel wanted Ramona to stay one more day, so Ramona **put off** ________.

a. dinner
b. her flight
c. her family
d. Vicente

B Match the words with their opposites.

h	1. rude	a. messy
____	2. healthy	b. relaxed
____	3. calm	c. get worse
____	4. greet	d. lie
____	5. admit	e. sick
____	6. well-organized	f. anxious
____	7. uneasy	g. say good-bye
____	8. improve	h. polite

C Match the expressions with the definitions.

__i__ 1. break up
____ 2. get along with
____ 3. check in
____ 4. pay attention to
____ 5. cheer up
____ 6. pick out
____ 7. depend on
____ 8. pick up
____ 9. drop by
____ 10. put off
____ 11. drop out of
____ 12. run into
____ 13. find out
____ 14. take care of

a. watch; be careful
b. meet someone by chance
c. watch; supervise
d. have a good relationship
e. register for an airplane flight
f. rely on; trust
g. leave; stop attending (usually school)
h. learn new information
i. end a relationship
j. meet someone (usually with a car)
k. change something to a later date
l. visit without calling first or without an invitation
m. make someone happier
n. choose

D Circle the two-word verbs and verb-preposition combinations in the puzzle. You can find words horizontally, vertically, diagonally, or backwards. The first word is done for you. Answers are on page 123.

```
O D A C N O E C N C T O A
T H C D U A L O E U N D T
N G T P N G O O D D K Y A
O T N I N U R E R N U B D
I T K C W O U O O O P P P
T K O K T G P D N H N O B
N P N O K O N T U C K R Y
E C N U U E P O H O E D N
T O H T P R F E L A I P E
T F O E R A C E K A T R P
A F D O E K F U O D T N P
Y B I C I R P P R P D E R
A F I N D O U T I I N U G
P I C K U P P P U T O F F
```

Lifeskill Practice

Job responsibilities

Ramona owns a business, and she and her employees work very hard. Here are some words we use to talk about being responsible at work.

A **Complete the information about Ramona's florist shop. Use the phrases in the box.**

depends on	**gets along with**	**pays attention to**
finds out	**knows how to**	**takes care of**

Ramona owns a florist shop. There are many things that Ramona ______________ at her business. Ramona ______________ her employees, but she ______________ them to get to work on time and to work hard. Ramona ______________ all the details of orders: the date, the amount, and the delivery time. She ______________ exactly what her customers want. Ramona ______________ make the best flower arrangements for her customers. That is why her business is successful.

B **Talk with a classmate about a person you know. Talk about the person's job. Use the words from Exercise A.**

Dialogue Practice

Practice the conversation with five classmates.

Lourdes: Vicente! We didn't expect to run into you today. Would you and your family like to join us for lunch? We're celebrating my birthday, a few months late.

Luis: Hi! You're the lady in the plaza. Don't you remember, Grandpa?

Vicente: I'm sorry, Mrs. Cruz. Let me introduce my daughter. Lupe, these are some old friends from San Antonio, Mrs. Lourdes Cruz, and her daughters, Isabel Molina and Ramona Rivera. This is Ramona's son, Ernesto.

Lupe: Oh, I remember you. You came into my shop yesterday, didn't you? I think you bought a lily.

Ramona: Oh, yes. You look familiar. That's a very nice shop. My mother is enjoying her lily.

Claudia: I'm Claudia Walker, a friend of the family. We met yesterday in the plaza. How nice to see you again.

Vicente: I'm sorry, Mrs. Cruz. We are a little late. We're going to have a quick lunch and leave. Claudia and I have to go to a meeting this afternoon. Please, have a nice birthday.

Answer Key to Episode 11 Word Search